ALLY MCCOIST

RANGERS LEGENDS

ALLY McCOIST

ALLY McCOIST with CRAWFORD BRANKIN

MAINSTREAM
PUBLISHING

EDINBURGH AND LONDON

This edition produced exclusively for
Rangers Football Club

First published in Great Britain in 1992 by
MAINSTREAM PUBLISHING COMPANY (EDINBURGH) LTD
7 Albany Street
Edinburgh EH1 3UG

This edition produced exclusively for Rangers Football Club 2001

ISBN 1 84018 539 2

A catalogue record for this book is available from the British Library

Printed and bound in Great Britain by
Cox and Wyman Ltd

CONTENTS

INTRODUCTION

Ally McCoist has one outstanding ability among the many football talents that he possesses, that is the ability to stick the ball in the back of the opposition's net with monotonous regularity. At a time when prolific goalscorers are becoming an endangered species, and when talented young players are having their originality coached out of them by a system which seems to have 'lost the place' a little, this comes as a breath of the freshest Scottish mountain air.

Not only is Ally McCoist a great player, in the mould of Law, Jim Baxter and Kenny Dalglish, he is also a clean, fair-minded player.

He is handsome, he is rich, he is funny and he is happy. He is a very popular person, even with me, and although I count him among my friends and wish him all the best, my envy knows no bounds.

Billy Connolly

Chapter One

GOALS, GOALS, GOALS

ANDY KNOX, quick and nimble as ever, started the move with a good ball out to Jack Kerr on the left. He was a really tricky winger – fast and elusive – and he sent in a brilliant cross over the head of the left-back. I ran on to it at the edge of the box, hit it as hard as I could, and the ball went in off the post. Ally McCoist, goalscorer had arrived. I was nine years old.

It was my debut for my local under-12s team, Calderwood Star and that was the first goal I can remember scoring. I remember too that I went fairly berserk when I scored it, which shows you that nothing has changed much through the years.

Goals . . . I've scored my share and done my fair share of enjoying them. Goals in England . . . goals for Rangers . . . goals for Scotland.

I've had some great moments on and off the park, but it has not all been plain sailing. Mixed in with the happy memories I'll never forget are some instances I only wish I could erase from the memory bank.

But I'm rushing things. Let's go back to 1971 and a very excited nine-year-old who had just scored a goal in East Kilbride . . .

Chapter Two

THE EARLY DAYS

ALBERT ENGLAND ran the Calderwood Star under-12 team in my native East Kilbride and was used to being pestered by would-be superstars who wanted a game in his side. But even he was taken aback when his doorbell sounded one day and yours truly was standing on his doorstep.

'Can I play in your team?' I wanted to know. I was seven years old, which goes to prove I was totally lacking in shyness even in those days.

Albert, to his credit, told me to come back when I was bigger. If I was good enough, I would get a game. He was a man of his word. So there I was two years later making my debut for Calderwood Star against arch East Kilbride rivals Villa Star.

I was still two years younger than most of the rest of the players so I was wearing the No. 7 shirt and told to operate in the comparative safety of the right-wing area. But I had a powerful incentive to make sure I got in among the action and the goals – my father Neil had promised me five pence a goal and I aimed to cash in.

Well, I described that first five pence worth on the previous page . . . and there were more to come. I finished with a hat-trick, we won 3-2 and I was 15 pence richer. Was that my amateur status at risk?

My dad actually kept that money-for-goals incentive going right through my school football days. In fact, I even managed to persuade him to take account of inflation and increase it to ten pence a goal after a while.

Looking back I was tremendously lucky in the help and encouragement I received from all quarters in those early days. My parents couldn't have been better. My dad actually ran Calderwood Star after I had been playing for them for a couple of years. But far from getting preferential treatment, I got more than my fair share of stick to ensure my feet were kept firmly on the ground. And my mum, Jessie, was in a different class. Our house was the team canteen and dormitory rolled into one. Team-mates would come back to be fed and to stay the night and they were always made welcome.

I hit it lucky with teachers too. The headmaster at my primary school in East Kilbride, Maxwellton, was a Mr Petrie. He used to take the team and referee our matches.

I remember we were playing our local rivals St Kenneth's in a League decider. We had to win to clinch the League, but a draw would give them the title. With a few minutes left, the score was 3-3 and I had one of those long-range blooters that you see in schools football. It bounced twice and then once more . . . right over their keeper. 4-3 to us. We had won the League. We were in the dressing-room celebrating, when one of their teachers came in to see Mr Petrie, who had been refereeing the game as usual. Their teacher had brought a spectator with him who said that our late-winner, my long-range effort, had in fact gone over the bar not under it and the goal shouldn't count. Mr Petrie didn't even hesitate. 'All right. It wasn't a goal,' he said. 'The game finished 3-3. Well done.'

Well, we were absolutely raging in the dressing-room. But he wasn't all that interested in winning or losing. He just wanted to see the boys running about, getting a game. That was the important thing to him.

That was a great attitude to instil in youngsters, and one that made sure we enjoyed our football. I think there's nothing worse than watching a kids' game with parents or teachers or whatever standing on the touchlines screaming abuse at their players. It's meant to be a fun game at that age.

Oh, and one more thing, Mr Petrie. Looking back, I've got

a feeling that shot of mine did go over the bar, although it's taken me 20 years to finally admit it.

When I went on to senior school in East Kilbride, Hunter High, I landed lucky again. The teacher who took the football there was the chemistry master, Archie Robertson, the former Clyde player and manager. Archie was a great, great man. He was suffering terribly from arthritis by this time, so much so that after soccer training in the gym we used to have to help him tie his shoelaces somedays. But his football brain was still razor sharp.

I remember he had us taking short corners. That seems nothing nowadays, but for a school team to do that in those days was really very innovative. He devised unusual exercises for sharpening our skills. We used to stand in two lines and really blast the ball at each other. It sounds crazy, but it meant we had to have quick reactions to survive the exercise and that paid off in game situations.

We were doing that particular exercise one day when one of the lads, who packed a real thump, caught Archie full in the face with the ball. There was a stunned silence as we waited for his reaction, then he just burst out laughing.

He didn't play favourites either. Although I was moving on in the game, that didn't get me any special favours. On the contrary, he was never off my back sometimes. But that wasn't a bad thing. It really used to exasperate him if I didn't play to my potential, but his criticism was always well intended. As my mum and dad both noticed, he never shirked the bad players. He was brilliant, and I was devastated when he died just before I left school.

Although football ruled my life, I wasn't averse to having a go at some other sports. My sister Alison was a first-rate handball player – she made the Great Britain team – and she got me interested in that. I was a bit smaller than your average handball player but I played a kind of link man role, shuttling between defence and attack.

I also had a go at rugby. I trained with the local team for around ten weeks and thoroughly enjoyed myself at their practice games. But I never played an actual full-scale match because of football commitments.

nd then there was swimming, scene of my first sporting
.. I came third in a school race to pick up a bronze medal and
I am convinced I would have landed gold but for an unfortunate
accident. My water wing fell off and I had to turn back for it. I
was six, and not really another David Wilkie in the making.

School studies were going fairly well, too. My sister Alison
is the brains of the family which she proved with a maths and
computing science degree. Some of that must have rubbed off on
me because I finished with a couple of Highers and seven 'O'
grades. That could have been better, I suppose, but studying was
never my strong point.

But then, of course, a lot was beginning to happen for me
on the football front. I had made the East Kilbride District side
and we reached the Scottish final against Aberdeen, who defeated
us 6–3 on the day . . . all their goals coming from a certain John
Hewitt. Incidentally, John and I have been good friends since that
day and I still think he is a vastly underrated player.

As well as turning out for Hunter High, I had moved on
from Calderwood Star to play for Fir Park Boys' Club. Roger
Hynd was Motherwell manager there at the time and was keen
to put me on an 'S' form, but I wasn't for signing anything like
that. I couldn't then, and still can't see the benefit of committing
yourself to a club with an 'S' form. It is great for the club . . .
they have the youngster well and truly tied up, but not so good
for the player himself. I've heard stories of boys who have signed
'S' forms and the managers haven't even bothered to register
them with the SFA, they've just stuck the completed form away
in a drawer somewhere.

I was also training with St Mirren some nights. Alex Ferguson was manager at Love Street then and he lived in East Kilbride.
He used to give four of us a lift over to training. One of the lads
was Steve Cowan. Fergie signed Steve on an 'S' form and he
eventually followed him up to Aberdeen when he went north.
He went on to Hibs and then Motherwell.

Fergie didn't offer me 'S' forms, which didn't bother me,
because I wouldn't have signed them anyway. To my mind I was
training and playing with Saints' 'S' forms and trialists and was
getting all the benefits they had, but I was free to go and play
where I liked.

I remember I played for a Saints side against Eastercraigs. I had a fair game and scored a goal, but Fergie still didn't approach me and soon after that he was away from Love Street and then off to Pittodrie. He has never told me directly why he didn't make me an offer, but I've heard through other sources that he thought I was too small.

It didn't really matter, because on the scene came St Johnstone. Their Glasgow scout Alex McLintock had been watching me and he drove me up to Perth to play a couple of trial games. Once again, if I'd been on 'S' form to, say, Motherwell, I couldn't have played these games at St Mirren or St Johnstone and would have missed out on a lot of experience.

Anyway St Johnstone were impressed, and they wanted to sign me . . . on semi-professional terms. Their manager, Alex Stuart, was straightforward and to the point. He promised me regular reserve football with the first team just round the corner. I liked him. I liked the place. I liked the idea of senior football and I went off to think things over for a few days.

Then, just when I had decided to say yes to Alex Stuart, Rangers contacted me. Their scout, George Runciman, had watched a Lanarkshire Schools Cup-tie with Hunter High against St Ambrose of Coatbridge. It finished 5-5, with me scoring four of our goals and having a hand in the fifth.

George phoned me up and asked would I go to Ibrox and have a chat with Willie Thornton. I'd like to set the record straight on this matter. There have been a lot of stories put about that I knocked back a fabulous Rangers signing offer to go to St Johnstone. Not true. At no time was there any mention of signing for Rangers at this stage. They wanted to talk, but what that chat would have entailed I never found out. I headed for Perth.

The lure of regular senior football every Saturday was a strong one. I was only 16, still at school, but I felt my game would develop better in that atmosphere than anywhere else and signed semi-professional forms at Muirton Park on St Andrew's Day, 1978. My signing fee? The princely sum of £150.

I was Ally McCoist of St Johnstone.

Chapter Three

PERTH: GATEWAY TO
THE BIG TIME

WHY St Johnstone? I wish I'd a fiver for every time someone has asked me that in the past ten years.

I suppose to the outsider it was an unusual choice. There I was, a West of Scotland boy, with any number of top-class clubs within easy distance of my home, choosing to travel at least three times a week halfway to the Highlands. But it made sense to me. I loved every minute of it.

St Johnstone was a really good club with its own special atmosphere. The park was tremendous, the dressing-rooms were big and well-equipped. The tearoom lady, Mrs Gibson, big Aggie's predecessor, looked after us as if we were her own. And the lads I travelled up from Glasgow with made the journey pass in no time. They were a great bunch – a mixture of seasoned professionals and up-and-coming youngsters like myself.

I may have been the 16-year-old still at school and going for 'O' grades and Highers but all the educational qualifications wouldn't have made me as streetwise as these guys. There were names like John Pelosi, Tam McNeill, Danny Scullion, Pat Conner, Dinghy Hamilton, Jackie O'Brien. Good fun, great company and quick to play a joke on unsuspecting youngsters, as I found out to my cost.

I fell asleep on the journey north one day and as the train pulled into Perth station, they crept out on to the platform as quietly as possible. When I had little or no time to get off the coach they started banging on the window to wake me up. I woke from a deep sleep, saw those faces and the Perth station sign outside the window, grabbed my kit to rush for the door and fell flat on my face. They had tied my shoelaces round the leg of the carriage table. By the time I had recovered, disentangled my feet and made it out of the carriage, they were rolling about the platform. It was Jackie O'Brien who had tied my laces together. I'd love to say I got my revenge, but I think I still owe him one.

And no wonder I was falling asleep on the journey. The two training nights per week were real marathons. I'd go straight from school to my mother's work in East Kilbride, where I'd grab a couple of rolls before catching the bus into Glasgow. The train left at 5.35 and got into Perth round 6.45. A taxi up to the ground, a hard training session, then the journey in reverse back home . . . arriving in East Kilbride just before midnight. That's dedication for you.

I had only one uneasy moment in my time at Perth and that came early on. I was getting changed in the away dressing-room with the rest of the reserves, when we heard this commotion out in the corridor. I looked out and saw Dinghy Hamilton and manager Alex Stuart having a real set-to. Words had obviously been said, but now it was getting far more serious. Dinghy was for taking on the world, and Drew Rutherford, the captain, and Doug Houston, the trainer, were trying to keep him and the boss apart.

For a 16-year-old just out of the relative calm of school and boys' club football, it was quite a shock. I remember thinking, 'What have I signed for here?' But it blew over quickly and life got back to normal at Muirton Park.

I had been promised regular reserve football and first team games if the opportunity arose. And that big chance nearly came a lot sooner than even I had anticipated. Saints had to play a Cup-tie against Morton and had real injury problems. I was down to play, but the match was postponed. The same thing happened again and again. By the time it did go ahead, the first team squad was back to full strength and A. McCoist was back to the reserves.

But I didn't have too long to wait for that first team debut.

Five months after signing I played in the top side against Raith Rovers. We won 3-0 and I had a hand in the second goal scored by Pat Ward who was also making his first appearance.

The following season saw a mixture of reserve and first team appearances. I think I played just over a dozen games with the big boys, but I was learning all of the time.

The next again season, 1980-81, was the real breakthrough. For a start I scored my first goal for St Johnstone in August when we beat Dumbarton at Boghead. We had a new boss by then – Alex Rennie had replaced Alex Stuart – and he decided on a different role for me. Instead of playing midfield as I had been for most of my football career up until then, he pushed me up front to partner John Brogan . . . and what a favour he did me with that move.

John Brogan was a magnificent striker. I was not at all surprised to see he was still banging in the goals for Stirling Albion late in his career. I learned so much just playing beside him. He taught me how a striker, more than any other player, has to think quickly. He could see an opportunity before it had happened, and when it did happen his reactions were like lightning. You can coach someone all you like, but that kind of killer instinct comes naturally or not at all.

By now, things were going really well for me. I was a first team regular with Saints, hitting the back of the net consistently and gaining recognition at a higher level. I had been picked for the Scottish semi-professional squad that went to Holland for a four-nation tournament against England, Italy and, of course, the Dutch. Jock Stein, then international manager, was there, and the squad was packed with top-class players from mostly the First Division – lads like Sandy Clarke, Gerry McCabe and Jamie Fairley.

I didn't play at all in the tourney, but we won it, and the celebrations were something else. And incidentally you can imagine that big, brash Amsterdam was a real culture shock to an East Kilbride boy, fresh out of school. Talk about an eye-opener!

School had given way to a business studies course in Hamilton, but that course was doomed to failure. At the end of the term I had to choose between sitting my exams or going with the Scottish Professional Youth squad to Monaco. It was no contest.

What a squad we took to Monaco for that tourney. Andy Roxburgh was in charge and his back-up was my Ibrox gaffer, Walter Smith, but a dark-haired Wattie, not the one who looks like Gene Pitney's double now! And among the players were Neale Cooper, Eric Black, Ian Ferguson, Davie Bowman, Gary Mackay, Nicky Walker and David Kenny.

In the end it turned out to be one of those glorious failures that Scottish teams have come up with down the years. After two of our three section games, we played the decider against France. We had to win to qualify, they only needed a draw to go through.

Well, I thought we'd done it when I scored 12 minutes from time to put us one up, but the French came back and equalised with literally the last touch of the game – their big centre-half heading home. I can still see it now in my mind's eye. Our dressing-room was gutted at full-time. I don't mind admitting I cried my eyes out. I couldn't believe football could be so cruel.

On a lighter note, that trip was memorable for a joke I played on Wattie Smith. He was doing a room check and when he went to have a look from our balcony I locked him outside. At first he saw the joke and I could see him laughing through the glass of the door. But the longer I left him out there, the less he saw the humour in the situation, and suddenly his eyes went very angry indeed.

Well, I just lost my bottle totally, threw down the key on the floor so that someone else could let him in and ran for my life. I stayed out of his way for a couple of hours until he had calmed down. Mind you, somedays at Ibrox now, when he is giving me a hard time, I wish I had left him on that balcony for good.

Back in Scotland my career was really hotting up. An STV film unit, in Perth for a different reason, filmed our game against Berwick. We won 6-2, with yours truly grabbing four goals. And when St Johnstone made a great start to season 1981-82 with good performances against Celtic, St Mirren and Hibs, and I scored in every one of those games, transfer talk was rife.

I had signed a new contract with St Johnstone but part of

that deal was the promise that they wouldn't stand in my way if a good offer came around. Along with Chairman Alex Lamond and Alex Rennie, my dad and I were invited down to look around Wolves, then Middlesbrough, then the one that really impressed me – Sunderland. The set-up at Roker Park was magnificent. They played to big crowds and their manager Alan Durban knew what he wanted and where he was going. They made St Johnstone a very good offer. They made me a good offer. Saints were happy with the deal and then wham! In came Rangers . . .

Rangers were my boyhood team and playing for them had been a dream since as long as I could remember. Now this was a real poser. John Greig had a long chat with my dad and me and told us what he hoped to achieve at Ibrox and how I could be a part of it. What a chance for an 18-year-old.

But I had seen and been impressed with Sunderland, and until Rangers' sudden interest I had settled in my own mind that I was going there. Also St Johnstone were much more keen for me to go to Sunderland than to Rangers. There was more money on offer from Roker Park than Ibrox and they were much happier selling me to an English club rather than a Scottish rival.

I agonised for 24 nervous hours and then made my decision. I said 'Sorry' to John Greig and signed on at Roker Park on 25 August, 1981.

I was Ally McCoist of Sunderland.

Chapter Four

SOUTH OF THE BORDER

MY introduction to the hard, fast and no-nonsense world of English football was short, sharp and painful. I'd just come on as substitute for Sunderland in the opening League game of the season when my opposite number stopped me in my tracks with a real bone-crusher.

It was a very hard, but scrupulously fair tackle from my immediate opponent. His name? Terry Butcher of Ipswich! Out of the corner of my eye I saw the big man watching for my reaction, so I pretended I hadn't felt a thing, while I was silently checking that all my joints were still in working order.

But there I was, less than a week out of the Scottish First Division, playing at Ipswich against England's central defence of Butcher and Russell Osman, and loving every minute of it. Well, almost every minute of it!

I'd signed for Sunderland earlier that week and realised straight away how much my life had changed. There was a photocall on the pitch at Roker Park that day and when I saw all those pressmen waiting for me, I suddenly felt very wary.

You'll have gathered already that I don't exactly lack self-confidence, but this was something different. All of a sudden I realised just what it meant to be a big-money signing. I was arriving with a reputation and people would be expecting big things from me. Did I live up to these expectations? Well, the honest answer to that has to be 'no'.

Let me say straight away that I couldn't have asked for more from the Sunderland fans. I struck up a great rapport with them from that first game, and they stayed loyal to me right through my time there. When things began to go wrong and I was getting some stick from the local press, they were still fantastic to me and shared my ups and downs. When I eventually scored my first goal for Sunderland, after two months of trying, you could almost feel the fans' sense of relief, too. They realised how desperately I wanted to do well, and respected me for that.

I still get lots of letters from the area, and it's a funny thing, but I feel I still owe the Sunderland fans something. I sometimes think I should go back there one day, an older, better player, and maybe repay their faith in me with a few more goals.

But it all started so well. That day at Ipswich I set up a goal soon after I came on. The game finished 3–3 and I felt that I had played well. It's strange, but that opening match remains one of my best memories of my time there. Incidentally, I should add that at the end of the game, big Butch was the first to shake my hand and wish me all the best in English football.

I'd fitted quickly into the scheme of things at Roker Park and settled in well at the digs the club had provided. I shared a room with another young professional, John Cook. Like myself, Cookie was 18, and he had played international youth football too, but for England. He came from the Manchester area and went back there eventually to play for Stockport. He was a great friend and ally, but I was good for him too. He was a terrible man for the horses and I used to drag him out of the bookies after just one bet so that we could go and play snooker. I must have saved him a fortune.

Barry Venison who went to Liverpool, was my other great mate. They called us the Three Stooges in the dressing-room. I wonder why?

Apart from them, there was a good mixture of youth and experience in the team with old pros like Leighton James and Frank Worthington – what a character he was! There were fellow Scots like Tam Ritchie, Iain Munro and Gordon Chisholm and good fun lads like Shaun Elliot, Gary Rowell and Bob Hind-marsh.

Alan Durban was a great boss. He was always totally honest with me and I knew where I stood with him and what he wanted from me.

Looking back, I still can't explain why it didn't work out much better down there. Maybe at 18 I was just too inexperienced to handle all the demands on the park and equally inexperienced to know how to apply myself off the park to help my game. It's not that I didn't work hard in training, but perhaps I was concentrating on the wrong aspects of my game. I kept saying to myself, 'Keep working hard, it'll come right', when I should have been sitting down and asking myself, '*Why* is it not coming right?'

After a few months, I was in and out of the first team and finding it hard going. My frustrations boiled over in one game when we travelled to Leeds United. Mick Buckley, one of our midfielders, sent me clear. I rounded their keeper but put the ball just past the post from a tight angle. It should have been a goal, and no one knew that more than me. I was sick. Then I looked up and saw Buckley gesturing to our huge support. He made it clear to them that as far as he was concerned I was a class one plonker.

If he had waited and criticised me privately, I would have taken it. But this public humiliation was too much. I thought it was a terrible thing to do to a fellow pro. I didn't miss him at half-time when I left him in no doubt what I'd do if it ever happened again. It didn't, but the incident showed how the situation was getting to me.

I was pretty low, but worse was to come in my personal life. I came home to East Kilbride one weekend to find that my mum and dad had decided to split up. This was the first I knew that their marriage was in trouble, and I'm ashamed to say I wasn't much help to them at the time.

I was really upset, but for purely selfish reasons. I was too concerned at the hurt they were giving me to appreciate the pain they were going through themselves. When I look back at my reaction then, I really hate myself. I know now it was the best

25

thing they could have done. They are both far happier now. They keep in touch and I'm delighted for both of them.

Unfortunately, I wasn't equipped with that sort of understanding back in the early 1980s and it was a very depressed Ally McCoist who drove back to Sunderland that weekend. But just when I needed a lift, it arrived in the shape of a new addition to the Roker Park dressing-room. Sunderland signed Ian Atkins from Shrewsbury, and Cookie and I were given the responsibility of making him feel at home.

The Roker Chairman told us to take him for a meal and charge it to the club. He expected us to go for some modest snack, but we had other ideas – a slap-up meal with wine and all the trimmings in the best hotel in the town. The Chairman was furious. We'd virtually wiped out his transfer budget in one huge binge. 'Ackers' was most impressed and promptly moved into our digs.

He was a Brummie and a funny, funny man. Anyone who has ever suffered a practical joke at my hands has probably him to thank. He loved a joke, and I'd be forever fnding his false teeth in my cup of tea, and other such pleasantries.

He was always wary of being caught out himself though. I remember he loaned me his car one night and it was stolen from outside the pub where I'd parked it. I couldn't remember the car number to report it to the police, but when I phoned up Ackers to ask him, he wouldn't believe me, and refused to tell me the number. It wasn't until the police found the car abandoned two days later that he finally admitted to himself that it had been stolen. Until then, he thought it had been a gigantic wind-up.

On the field, too, things were looking up with Sunderland, and McCoist, off to a good start to the new season. After some goals in the pre-season friendlies, I was in the team for the opening match at Aston Villa. This was Villa's first game since they had lifted the European Cup and making his Villa debut that day was a young winger called Mark Walters, but we beat them 3-1 and I got a goal. I also got a clip on the ear from a member of the Midlands Constabulary for running off the park to celebrate that goal with the Sunderland fans who had made the trip.

That was the start of a good run for me and for the team. I followed the Villa goal by hitting the net at Everton and

Manchester City, both notoriously hard grounds to visit, and after 13 games I'd notched seven goals. Not bad, but not good enough. Alan Durban dropped me for a home match. I remember him explaining he wanted to freshen up the team and that was me back in the reserves.

Of course, the club had been changing over the two seasons. Players like Chris Turner, Nick Pickering and Colin West had been signed. There was a good young side in the making, competition for places was fierce, and I just had to take my first team chances if and when they came my way.

But I'd made an impression elsewhere in Sunderland! One weekend I met local girl Allison Mitchell and we were instantly attracted to each other. Allison was modelling in London and had come back to Sunderland for a weekend visit. That meeting was the start of a long-distance romance that eventually led to us becoming married at the end of 1990.

While Allison was working in London, I only saw her at weekends. That arrangement seemed set to change when she decided to quit the capital and come back to Sunderland. But things weren't to be that easy for us. No sooner had she arrived back than I was on the move. To this day, she says I did it deliberately!

It started when I reported for training and Alan Durban hit me with the stunning news: 'Rangers have made a bid for you.' I asked his advice and, as ever, he was honest and to the point. He said I should take the chance because he could see big changes happening at Sunderland, and they might not be for the best. He said he might even get the chop in the near future. As it happened he was right.

As I made the short drive to Carlisle to meet the Rangers management team of John Greig and Tommy McLean, I thought back over two seasons at Sunderland. I had come to England to learn, and I felt I had found out a lot about myself as a player and as a person. I had played at the biggest venues in England – Anfield, Old Trafford, Goodison, Highbury. I'd faced the very best – Robson, Dalglish, Hoddle, Brady. I'd scored goals against Peter Shilton and pierced the best defences in the country. I was no failure and I would prove that. I was going home to succeed.

On 8 June 1983, I signed for John Greig.

I was Ally McCoist of Rangers.

Chapter Five

MY FIRST MEDAL

WHEN I signed at Ibrox I thought Rangers were getting the finished article – the complete player. But I was wrong . . . very wrong. I still had an awful lot of growing up to do in many aspects of my play, and in my mental approach to the problems that cropped up.

I'd do silly things. Bad tackles would annoy me and destroy my concentration. Worst of all, I'd let missed chances worry me – and that would invariably lead to more missed chances. I know now that you have to put mistakes like that out of your mind and concentrate 100 per cent on what is happening now, not what might have been three minutes earlier. A little of that knowledge might have spared me – and the Rangers fans – some bad times back in the early '80s.

I had my moments, of course. I'd made my Ibrox debut in the opening League game of the season – a 1-1 draw with St Mirren. I didn't score then, but I did hit my first goal for the club soon after in a midweek League Cup tie at Queen of the South.

Then came Celtic at Parkhead. We'd played them pre-season in the Glasgow Cup final at Hampden, and won 1-0 thanks to a Sandy Clark goal, but that, by Old Firm standards, was pretty low key. This was different.

I'd never been more nervous before the start of a game. What I needed was an early touch to settle my nerves and I watched anxiously as Robert Prytz sent Davie McKinnon clear down the right in the opening seconds. He did very well to reach the ball at the byeline and whip in a low, hard cross. It came through a crowd of players straight to me and I stuck it away through Pat Bonner's legs.

Only 27 seconds had gone. It was, and still is, the fastest ever goal in an Old Firm game. It came at the Celtic end, too, and the Jungle watched, full of appreciation I'm sure, as I celebrated in true McCoist style. Mind you, the Parkhead fans had the last laugh on the day when a Frank McGarvey goal four minutes from time gave them victory. But that one of mine was the start of what has turned out to be a good scoring record against Celtic – and long may that continue.

But that defeat was one of a few bad results early in the League campaign and I was learning quickly of the unique pressures that Rangers players are under. At Sunderland it was bad if we lost, but not the end of the world. With Rangers it was a crisis if we only drew! The Rangers fans were desperate for success after a comparatively lean time, and they were quick to let that impatience show when results started to go against us. You could almost touch the tension on some match days.

Taking the brunt of the stick, of course, was manager John Greig and three months into the season he decided he'd had enough and quit. I can still vividly remember the scene in the dressing-room the day he told us. He'd known a lot of the squad for years and quite a few of the players were in tears on his behalf. I must admit I was a bit upset myself.

John Greig is a nice man, perhaps too nice a person for the cut and thrust of football management. I've heard it said that he didn't have the respect of the squad – particularly those he had played with – but that is nonsense as far as I'm concerned.

Sure there were moans behind his back, like: 'He forgets he was a player himself once . . . ' But to be fair, I've heard the same accusations levelled at Alan Durban and Graeme Souness from disgruntled players and it is just a part of dressing-room life. Greigy had a great knowledge of football and how he liked it to be played. I had total respect for him as a manager and as a person and I still do today. I'm delighted he's back at Ibrox in a public relations capacity now.

But in John Greig's place came Jock Wallace. The old hands

from his previous spell at the club warned me what to expect –
a big, hard, honest but fair man – and they were totally correct.
He set about righting what he thought was wrong with Rangers,
and missed no one.

Jock was a superb one-to-one motivator, singling out players
for dressing-room pep talks that left you in no doubt about
what was expected of you. And if you didn't live up to these
expectations you were in trouble.

I must certainly have failed some of these early Wallace tests.
He obviously didn't see A. McCoist as the answer to his goal-
scoring problems. One of his first moves was to try and sign
Nottingham Forest striker Ian Wallace. That failed but he then
snapped up Bobby Williamson from Clydebank to lead the line,
and I was bumped into the reserves. To add to my gloom I then
broke my wrist playing for the club in an indoor five-a-side
tournament in East Kilbride.

Worse was to follow. Jock pulled me into his office one day
to tell me that Sunderland had made a bid to buy me back. He
told me to go and think about it, and didn't advise me one way
or the other, but his manner suggested that it wasn't going to
break his heart if I said 'Yes' to another stint at Roker Park.

Looking back, this was probably the moment when my
career could have gone off the rails totally. An inglorious exit
from Sunderland was still a vivid memory, and now another
team seemed prepared to cut their losses and run as far as I was
concerned. My self-confidence, perhaps the strongest part of my
character, was in danger of collapsing totally. What had gone
wrong?

I remember sitting at home that night, arm in plaster, feeling
really sorry for myself. What should I do?

The easiest answer seemed to me to head back to Sunderland,
where I was wanted, rather than try and force my way back into
favour at Ibrox, where I might never be wanted again. But despite
some disappointments and the internal upheaval, I'd enjoyed
much of my few months at Ibrox. Rangers were all I'd imagined
them to be when I supported them as a boy. I was a Rangers
player, and I wasn't going to give that up without a fight.

I saw big Jock the next day and told him I wanted to stay.
I said I was sure I could make it at Ibrox and I was prepared to

wait and fight for my first-team place. He didn't say much, just gave me one of his hard stares and said, 'OK.' But deep down I think my attitude impressed him. Now I would have to make sure my play impressed him, too.

What did help in that area were the beneficial effects of the new-style training regime that the big man had started on his return. There is a lot of nonsense talked about big Jock grinding players mercilessly at training. And the pre-season visit to the Gullane sands is looked upon as some kind of never-ending torture. But although Jock wanted us fit and sharp, he gave us no more arduous work than John Greig did, or Graeme Souness did, and Walter does now. In fact, the first pre-season work in Italy with Souness and Smith was by far the hardest build-up I've ever done – much worse than any Gullane sands.

But what Jock was very keen on was upper body strength. Every day we used to do a weights circuit in the away dressing-room. It was a series of really punishing body exercises and they soon had a big effect on me. I became stronger and harder, and that physical edge helped my game. Under Jock I developed more than I had done in the previous six years. Maybe that's the way I was to grow up and it would have happened with or without Jock's help, but I felt stronger and more able to take care of myself in the rough and tumble of the penalty area, and I became a better player for having that physical edge.

I can't emphasise strongly enough how important this particular spell was to me. It might be a bit melodramatic to say it, but I think Jock Wallace saved my career at that time. I was at an awkward crossroads, and Jock was the perfect influence. John Greig might have been just as beneficial had he stayed around as manager. I'll never know. All I am sure of is that the Ally McCoist who emerged midway through the season 1983-84 was a more complete player than the one who'd started it.

I had stared potential failure full in the face and hadn't liked it one bit, so I'd done something about it. I'd grown up a bit. I still had some painful lessons to learn, but I was getting there.

And so were Rangers. A bad series of defeats had been halted and the team was enjoying a run of 20 unbeaten games, not enough to win the League after such a bad start, but a good way of restoring some credibility in the eyes of the fans. By the end of January, I'd forced my way back into the team, and was working well in attack with Sandy Clark – a good unselfish professional and the ideal foil for someone like myself.

While League form had been erratic, our League Cup displays had been superb and we had marched on convincingly to a final against Celtic. But just when we looked ideally placed for the big game, there came a huge setback. The week before the final we lost our unbeaten run when Dundee knocked us out of the Scottish Cup in a 3-2 replay at Ibrox. Worse still, Ian Redford had been sent off during the game, and Robert Prytz just after the final whistle, making them both ineligible for Hampden the following week. You can imagine how delighted big Jock was with the pair of them!

That midweek we travelled to Belfast for a testimonial game against Linfield. I played midfield and scored in our 3-0 win and I knew I was earmarked for a similar role in Sunday's final. Apart from that pre-season Glasgow Cup final, this was my first visit to Hampden.

What a day 25 March 1984 turned out to be. The teams that day were: *RANGERS*: McCloy, Nicholl, Dawson, McClelland, Paterson, McPherson, Russell, McCoist, Clark (McAdam), Mac-Donald (Burns), Cooper. *CELTIC*: Bonner, McGrain, Reid, Aitken, McAdam, MacLeod, Provan (Sinclair), P. McStay, McGarvey (Melrose), Burns, McClair.

Although Celtic just had the edge on us in League meetings that season, there was a real confidence about the Rangers dressing-room on the day. Big Jock didn't need to motivate any of us for this one. It just wasn't necessary. We were going to win.

As expected, I was playing right midfield, against Murdo MacLeod. And I did my job pretty well. I don't think I've ever won so many tackles in a match. That just shows how fired up I was.

After a fairly even start, we had the perfect end to the first half. Bobby Russell played a one-two with Davie Cooper, but Murdo MacLeod brought him down. A penalty, and I stuck it away to Pat Bonner's left. Then early in the second half came what I thought was the clincher. Sandy Clark nodded on a huge kick out from big Peter McCloy and I slid it under Bonner's body. 2-0 to us. Where was the champagne?

But all credit to Celtic. Brian McClair pulled one back for them fairly quickly, but we were holding out very comfortably, when I decided to have another say in the proceedings. With a minute to go, I challenged Murdo MacLeod in the box and Bob Valentine gave a penalty. Incidentally, I've watched the incident umpteen times on television since then and I know it looks like a foul, but I still maintain to this day that I touched the ball first. No-one believes me, and I don't suppose you lot out there will either, but I stick by my story. Not that my version mattered at the time. Bob Valentine stuck by his decision and Mark Reid stuck the penalty past big Peter. Final score 2-2. Hold the champagne.

We reshuffled the team for extra-time, with me moving up front. It quickly paid dividends. Roy Aitken whacked into me from the back as I tried to control a through ball. Another penalty, said Mr Valetine, and this time I agreed totally. (I've never yet been awarded a penalty I've disagreed with. Funny that!)

Up I stepped, confidently expecting to slot home the kick. But Pat Bonner obviously hadn't read the script. He blocked my first effort, but thankfully didn't hold it, and I was able to touch home the rebound. Talk about relief!

Well, that was the drama over for the day, but not the celebrations. I'd won my first senior football honour – by scoring a hat-trick in a Cup final against Celtic. That's a fair day in anyone's life, and it wasn't finished yet. The dressing-room scenes were incredible. After all the hassle and disappointment of the season, everyone just wanted to party.

I remember attending the post-match press conference with Bobby Russell who had turned in an absolutely brilliant performance. But although I always enjoy the banter of occasions like that, I was strangely uneasy at this one. I just wanted out of it and back in among the dressing-room madness. We were a team who had come through a lot together. We had won as a team. We were going to celebrate as a team.

We did, too, with big Jock at his ebullient best. Allison had come up from Sunderland for the game and was greeted straight after it with a typical Jock Wallace bear-hug. She swears he cracked about four of her ribs.

As the team coach headed back to Ibrox for the official party, I was delighted for all the Rangers fans who filled the streets. We had given them something to celebrate. And on a personal note, surely I had won them over once and for all to my side? Was that me finally and totally accepted by the Ibrox legions?

Not yet, as I was still to discover!

Chapter Six

DOWN AND ALMOST OUT

THE packed Copland Road stand rose as one voice and chanted my name. But this was no song of love. It was a hymn of hate.

'Ally, Ally get to ————. Ally, get to ————.'

It was 16 February 1985 – without a doubt the worst day in my football life and one that still makes me cringe when I think of it. Rangers were on their way to a 1-0 Scottish Cup defeat by Dundee. I was having a real stinker of a game and the Rangers fans were letting me know in no uncertain terms what they thought of my efforts.

But their reaction that day was the culmination of a very mixed season for the team in general and me in particular. Like the previous season, we had won the League Cup – an Iain Ferguson goal giving us a 1-0 win over Dundee United – but we couldn't find the consistency necessary to mount a real push for the title. As the season progressed we found ourselves further and further off the pace and the fans were growing more and more restless.

Like the team, I was pretty inconsistent myself. I was scoring some goals, playing quite well some games and not so well on other days. Unfortunately I had the unhappy knack of picking the really big occasion to make the memorable mistakes.

In the second round of the UEFA Cup we played Inter Milan and the game was televised live back home. They gave us a terrible thrashing that night and despite a magnificent goal by Karl Heinz Rummenigge being ruled off for dangerous play, they still thumped us 3-0. But when it was 2-0 I missed a great chance to bring us right back into the game. Ian Redford smacked in a tremendous shot which hit the bar and spun back in the air to me. Their keeper was still on the ground and I had an empty net to head into. But I jumped too early, met the ball when I was on the way down and the header missed.

After the game Peter McCloy tried to console me by saying that it would just have annoyed Inter if I'd scored and they'd just have run up the park and added some more. It was good of him to say that, but deep down I knew that if I'd made it 2-1, it would have put a whole new complexion on the game, and who knows what the final result would have been?

Anyway I took a lot of stick in the press and was dropped for the return game. Big Jock played centre-back John McClelland up front and his tactics nearly paid off. Rangers won 3-1. It wasn't enough, however. We were out of Europe, and I was in the reserves.

I could have been off down south again. My old Sunderland boss Alan Durban had moved on to Cardiff City by then and tried to buy me. Although I was out of favour at the time, big Jock knocked that one back, and I was glad. I wasn't for quitting, although some days it was very tempting.

Off the field I was getting more flack from Rangers fans than Celtic punters – and that was hard to take. Allison and I were walking in East Kilbride town centre one day when three young lads – all wearing Rangers scarves – started on me.

'Hey, McCoist. You are ––––––– useless. Away back to England.'

Allison was horrified. This had never happened in Sunderland. She wanted to stay and argue with them, and I had to calm her down.

Then another day we were in Glasgow's city centre and I heard this shout. 'Hey Ally!' That sounded quite friendly so we turned round and there were four men working on scaffolding, all making obscene gestures at me. A couple of them were wearing Rangers colours, too.

I just thought to myself what idiots four grown men,

probably with families, were making of themselves and tried to laugh it off, but they really got to Allison. She was very upset and it took a while to persuade her that only a small percentage of the population could be so moronic.

All in all, it was a hard time for my family and friends. Although outwardly I wasn't letting it get to me, those closest to me could sense the strain I was under. I could also see the stress on my mother's face sometimes, and a couple of my pals actually got in fights with their workmates defending me. It's a serious business this football, but worse was to come for them and me.

After a long spell in the reserves I had got a toehold back in the first team early in the New Year. With the League virtually gone, the Cup was the only realistic trophy left to chase that season and there was a good crowd at Ibrox that fateful February day.

We got the worst possible start when John Brown scored for Dundee after only nine minutes, but there was plenty of time left for us to get back at them. We proceeded to make chance after chance and I proceeded to miss them. Every opportunity fell to me. I put them over the bar, by the left-hand post, by the right-hand post, straight at the keeper. You name it. I did it.

I'd give up 20 of the other goals I've scored in my time at Ibrox just to have got one in the net that day, but it wasn't to be. I had a stinker, and I deserved to get some stick.

But did it merit that song of hate? I don't think so. I can't tell you how it feels to have a whole stand rising in unison against you. I can still feel almost physically sick when I recall it. I could be quite bitter about it, too. Nowadays when I get the backslapping and autograph requests from Rangers fans, I find myself thinking: 'Were you one of the chorus that day?' It is hard to push it to the back of my mind.

There were about ten minutes left when the song started and I remember staring at the turf and being conscious of the Dundee players around me just looking at me, watching for my reaction. John Brown, whom I'd known since schoolboy football days, came up to me with some words of encouragement. Of course, John was a real bluenose even then and couldn't believe what his goal had caused.

Anyway, the final whistle went and I headed for the dressing-room. I was sitting on my own trying to compose myself and I think I would have been alright if it hadn't been for coach John Hagart who came up to me, grabbed my hair and tried some words of comfort.

That just broke me. I burst into tears. The months of abuse and controlling my feelings took their toll and I howled like a baby. Outside the dressing-room I could hear the fans in Edmiston Drive shouting. The team was getting stick. I was getting stick. It wasn't a nice time.

The rest of the team went off to the bath, except for big Derek Johnstone and Colin McAdam. They sat waiting for me to compose myself and then came up and started chatting. They were just brilliant. Eventually they even had me managing a wry grin or two.

As we got dressed to go home, the mob outside were still howling for blood and Derek had some good advice for me. He warned me that when I went out the door the punters would be giving me stick. But I had to keep my head down and not stop walking till I reached my car. On no account was I to stop and start arguing with them. That would be fatal.

Out I went to a really hot reception. I was all the useless so and sos under the sun, but I made it to the car where Allison was waiting along with her aunt and uncle. They were making their first trip north to see me playing. What a welcome to Ibrox!

But as we sped off I glanced back and saw that big Derek and Colin hadn't quite practised what they preached. They had stopped and were arguing furiously with some punters on my behalf.

Jock Wallace defended me too in the press by reminding Rangers fans that less than a year before I had scored a hat-trick to win the League Cup, but it didn't seem to have much effect on the nutters who wrote to me. That week I got some real hate mail – sick letters from sick people – but to balance that I received a marvellous letter from Willie Woodburn.

I'd never met him at that time (and still haven't for that matter) but he wrote and told me to forget all that had happened the previous week. He thought that I'd all the makings of a great player and that one day I'd prove all these fans wrong. Getting a letter like that from a real Rangers legend was a tremendous lift – at a time when I really needed it. I can't thank him enough for that.

The next week I was dropped for the match at Tynecastle and I was very unhappy. I spoke to big Jock and told him that I thought he was giving in to all the pressure by leaving me out. But he was adamant that he wanted me to play in the reserves and get my confidence back. I was really angry at that, but I now realise he was doing me a favour. I played in the stiffs that weekend and scored a goal, but the top team lost 2-0 to Hearts. If I had played in that and had another nightmare, I might never have come back.

But come back I did and in quite spectacular style. Don't ask me why or how it happened, but if I have to pinpoint a time when things began to really click for me at Ibrox then it has to be from there on in. I had only scored one League goal for Rangers all season, but in the ten remaining games from the beginning of March that season I notched eleven. And as the goals began to go in with a bit more regularity, the rest of my play improved too.

And the fans noticed. During that run-in, we played Celtic at Parkhead. Both teams were out the League race – well behind Aberdeen – but there is no such thing as a meaningless Old Firm match. It turned into a real rough-house. There were plenty of bookings and we had Davie Cooper and Ally Dawson sent off as we trailed by an Alan McInally goal. Incredibly nine-man Rangers came back into the game and late on we got a penalty when big Roy Aitken handled. It was at the Rangers end of the ground, and I've never known pressure like it.

I've taken penalties in Cup Finals and in Europe, but I can never remember being as nervous as I was that night at Parkhead. Two months ago I was the villain of the piece at Ibrox. What if I messed this one up? I took a couple of deep breaths, swallowed hard and rammed the penalty past Pat Bonner to give us a 1-1 draw.

I was pounded by my delirious team-mates but over and above their congratulations I heard a new song from the massed ranks of Rangers fans. It wasn't too tuneful, but it was sweet music to my ears. They were giving it 'Super Ally'.

I had arrived.

Chapter Seven

ALL CHANGE AT IBROX

I WAS the first Ibrox player to know that Jock Wallace was about to be sacked by Rangers. That came from big Jock himself only a couple of weeks before the axe fell on him in April 1986. In mid-March he called me into his office to talk about my own future. My contract was up at the end of the season and he was keen that I should stay on at Ibrox.

By this time, Jock and I were very close. I got my bawlings out, the same as everyone else, but he would also confide in me about his hopes and plans. That day started out as a discussion about my future, but soon switched to his long-term Ibrox ambitions. He wanted to sign three players – Gordon Durie, then of Hibs, John Brown and Craig Levein. He felt that Durie and I would be a good team up front and that it would be in my interest to stay with Rangers and be a part of it. But he added ominously that the board were proving a bit sticky in agreeing to spend that type of cash. And he joked that if they didn't agree to give him the money it was a sure sign that he would be shown the door. Neither of us realised how prophetic his words were to be.

The season had started so well for us, too. After six League games we were top of the table with five wins and one draw. But then we won only two of our next ten Championship games and were virtually out of the title race by New Year.

The annoying thing was that, personally speaking, I was playing my best stuff for Rangers to date. I was scoring goals consistently, my general game was in fine shape too, and I was mentioned in the press as a possible Scotland player. What a change in a year!

Agents from Belgium and Spain had contacted me about the possibility of going abroad when my contract was up and Everton were strongly tipped to be chasing me. But I was desperate to win more honours with Rangers. Unfortunately, this season wasn't to provide any. We had lost to Hibs in the League Cup semi-final, had been knocked out of Europe in the first round by Osasuna of Spain and Hearts had banged us out of the Scottish Cup early on as well. To make matters worse, we were so far down the League that we weren't even guaranteed a place in Europe next season – that still had to be clinched.

But the final crunch for Jock came when we lost 2-0 to Spurs in a friendly at Ibrox. We were disgraceful that day. The whole side owes Jock an apology for the performance then, but judging by what he'd hinted at to me a couple of weeks earlier, nothing we could have done was really going to save him from the chop.

I was down in Sunderland the following day when my mother phoned me at tea-time with the bombshell news – Jock had been fired and the new manager was to be Graeme Souness.

My first reaction was to feel absolutely gutted for big Jock. As I explained, we had become very close and although I never got the chance to hear his farewell at Ibrox, I went round to his house in Bothwell as soon as I came back north to see him and his wife Daphne and wish them both all the best.

The dressing-room the next morning was a strange mixture of gloom and tension. There was genuine sympathy for what had happened to big Jock, but a tingle of excitement as to what lay round the corner for the club. We knew we were getting a great player in Graeme Souness. He was an unknown force as a manager, but on the field he would be an incredible asset. There was the knowledge, too, that in going to get a player of his stature and calibre the club must be aiming very high indeed.

Chairman David Holmes then entered the dressing-room with our new player-boss who spoke to the entire playing staff. My first impression was of the immediate presence of the man. He was dressed immaculately; he looked fit and tanned and he spoke with firm authority. He said that he was used to success and he wanted to bring success to Rangers. Everyone on the staff would have the chance to show what they could do and he was looking forward to working with us as a team. Straight to the point – short and sweet.

It was a strange period, because our new player-manager then had to go back to Italy to fulfil his contract with Sampdoria and wouldn't be free to join us until the last game of the season. But before then Walter Smith arrived from Dundee United to be the new assistant manager and I got the first taste of what life might be like under the new regime.

We still needed some points to be sure of a European place the following season and didn't do our case any good by losing 2-1 at St Mirren. I didn't play well and got an absolute roasting in the dressing-room at full-time from Wattie. He told me that from now on, scoring goals wouldn't be enough. They'd be looking for a lot more elsewhere from me as well.

But the good news was that, like big Jock before them, the new bosses were keen for me to sign a new contract with Rangers. And despite the nibbles from elsewhere, I was every bit as keen to stay.

Graeme Souness duly took over on 3 May and I scored a penalty in our 2-0 win over Motherwell – the victory that guaranteed us a European place the following year.

There were only two unfinished bits of business left for the season – the Glasgow Cup final against Celtic the following Friday night and my new contract. We decided both would be dealt with at the same time. I was meant to meet the manager and chairman before the game and hopefully sign the new deal before kick-off. But the interest in the match was phenomenal and I got held up in traffic. By the time I got to Ibrox there was no time to talk business and the manager was not pleased with me at all.

However, I went out on the park and scored a hat-trick as we beat Celtic 3-2, so I felt he couldn't really complain. On the contrary, he still thinks I timed it all deliberately, so the club would have to increase their offer to me.

After the game I went upstairs to the manager's office where he and the chairman and secretary Campbell Ogilvie were waiting with the contract. When other players go to these negotiations, they have agents and financial advisers with them. I don't. I was there on my own.

But I had just scored a hat-trick against Celtic in a Cup final. I was still on a high and decided I'd have a little fun at their expense. The terms on the contract were read out to me. They really were fantastic, but just for a laugh I said, 'Sorry, I'm not signing'.

I can still see the three chins dropping in amazement and the look of disbelief on their faces sent me into a fit of the giggles. Scoring Cup-final hat-tricks really is a heady mixture.

There was a long silence, broken only by my laughter, then eventually the chairman realised what was going on. 'Ally, it's been a long day,' he said. 'Would you just sign this and let me get to my bed.'

Rangers and Graeme Souness were going places. No way was I going to miss out. I signed.

Chapter Eight

A WHOLE NEW BALL GAME

THE minute Graeme Souness walked through the door at Ibrox he set in motion a chain of events that totally changed the shape of Rangers Football Club and possibly Scottish football itself.

Rangers had always been a big club with the potential to be an even bigger club. Now there were no ifs about it. They *were* going to be the biggest. Overnight everything was on a grander scale. Crowds went up. Media interest rocketed. We were playing for bigger stakes. We had thrown down a challenge to the rest of football and we couldn't slip up.

My old Sunderland team-mate Colin West arrived to partner me up front. Then Chris Woods and, unbelievably, Terry Butcher. The man meant business.

Pre-season training was different, too. The manager was keen on improving our suppleness as well as our fitness, so every training stint was preceded with a long period of stretching exercises. We got dietary advice, and were encouraged to eat high-energy foods like pasta. He was thorough and detailed in all such matters.

And on the park, it was to be a whole new ball game. We were going to play 100 per cent football right through the team. No more hopeful long punts up the park. Instead our back men were to play it about until they saw an opening. The midfield were to get involved and we were to run and work hard up front making the openings for them to hit. The manager was quick to appreciate just how new this was to so many of us. But he was determined that this was how we would play and he hadn't a lot of time to get it right.

We went on a pre-season visit to Europe to put his theories into practice and it was fascinating stuff. I think we learned very fast. I know we had a few upsets but I still maintain the football we played in the first half of season 1986-87 is the best of any side in my career. We were a good solid team from goalkeeper to number 11 and we were trying to play football and succeeding most of the time.

Souness had this ability to spot the potential pass before it was on and hit it at the perfect moment. In midfield with the boss was Ian Durrant, by then the best young midfielder in Britain, and scoring goals as well as making them.

Big Colin West had taken a bad knee injury early in the season and I'd been teamed up front with Robert Fleck, the start of a partnership that was to net something like 60 goals between us. I feel sorry for big Westie, the way things worked out we never really got a chance to prove if we could have hit it off. By the time he was back to fitness Robert and I were well established as the front team.

Right up to the moment he left the club, I never felt Robert was given the credit he deserved by the fans. He was a far better player than many realised. He had great pace, and everyone recognised that. But on top of that he was brave, unselfish and a very good finisher. I thought we struck up a good understanding from the word go, but, as I said earlier, the service we were getting from midfield was pretty special.

And every so often we enjoyed a special pass or two straight from defence, courtesy of big Butch's lethal left peg. I nicknamed his left leg 'The Winchester' because he could ping a pinpoint accurate pass a tremendous distance, but that of course is only one aspect of his game.

I can't emphasise enough how important Terry Butcher has been to all that has happened at Rangers in recent years. As well as his abilities on the park, he really was a superb captain and motivator. His presence and influence in the dressing-room before a game was . . . awesome. There's no other word for it. He is a big man and when he shouted at you you listened. He wanted to win all the time whether it was a cup final or a silly five-a-side at training. Having him as your skipper was sometimes like having an extra man in your team. It was like walking on to the field of battle behind Robert the Bruce, although I don't know if he'll appreciate that comparison.

And of all the new faces at Ibrox the man who most appreciated our initial success was big Butch. That came in a League Cup final which was full of drama and controversy. After an early fright at East Fife, when we'd scraped by on penalties, we had stormed through the League Cup, improving with every round and defeating Dundee United decisively in the semi-final to set up an October final with Celtic. We'd beaten Celtic earlier in the season in a televised league game at Ibrox – Ian Durrant scoring a magnificent winner – and the tension and commitment on the field that day had brought home to all the new faces at Ibrox just what an Old Firm game means to the city.

Until then, I don't think the manager had quite realised the enormity of the job that bossing Rangers had become. He had been quoted as saying that an Old Firm game was just another two points, but he learned then it was much more than that. Now here we were with an Old Firm final. I don't think it will ever go down as one of the Old Firm classics, but we certainly weren't complaining.

Ian Durrant shot us ahead in the second half, but Brian McClair hammered home a fine equaliser. Then came the moment of drama when Roy Aitken pulled back big Butch in the Celtic area and referee David Syme gave a penalty. Davie Cooper slotted it home, but Celtic weren't happy at all. Mo Johnston was sent off soon afterwards and for a while it looked as if Tony Shepherd was going to join him as things were getting out of hand. Eventually it calmed down and we had won the League Cup. I'll never forget big Butch's face that afternoon as we went on the lap of honour. He was loving every minute of it and who could blame him?

That night we went back to Ibrox for a party. As usual the players and their wives and girlfriends were joined by all the people who work at the stadium – from the cleaners to the tea ladies. I think it is a marvellous idea which shows the spirit which runs through the club.

After a few drinks there, Allison and I and Stuart Munro and his wife Carolyn headed off to town with Doddie, the kit man, to join the rest of the players at a special disco. When we got there, one of our team was already on the dance floor – a bottle of champagne in each hand singing at the top of his voice the chant: 'There's only one Terry Butcher.'

The songster? Big Terry himself . . . and we all joined in.

Chapter Nine

CHAMPIONESE

THE League Cup was standing proudly in the Ibrox trophy
room. It looked great, but everyone at Ibrox realised that was
only the beginning. We all knew that the big target still lay
ahead . . . the Premier League Championship. We hadn't won
the title since Jock Wallace's treble team of 1978. We had come
close on a couple of occasions but had dropped out of the running
far too quickly in other years. It had to be different this season,
but, boy, it was going to be difficult – we knew that right from
the word 'go'.

The Championship season began with the infamous battle
of Easter Road. We lost 2-1 to Hibs; Graeme Souness was sent
off in his first ever Scottish League game; and both clubs were
eventually punished by the SFA for their overall behaviour.

It was the worst possible start for the manager and all he
was trying to achieve at Ibrox. He'll be the first to admit that his
clash with George McCluskey was wrong and he deserved to be
punished for it. But in my opinion some very inflammatory
shouts from McCluskey right at the beginning of the match went
a long way to creating the atmosphere on the park that day.

It certainly was one of the nastiest games I've ever played
in. And I'm not proud of my own behaviour at all that day. But
I've never – and I mean never – seen a team so fired up against
us as Hibs were that afternoon. And I've played in some hard,
no-nonsense games in my time.

Graeme Souness had arrived at the end of the previous season and sparked off the biggest media circus Scottish football had ever seen. All summer long Rangers had been in the news as the big signings arrived and everyone looked forward to seeing the new-look Light Blues in competitive action for the first time.

Eventually the talking had to stop and all the hype that had gone before went against us. The world was waiting to knock us off our pedestal. And although it was never as bad as that day at Easter Road, there were many other occasions when we came up against teams who were unbelievably fired up to bring us down a peg or two.

Hate is a very strong word, and I don't use it lightly, but I do believe that in some quarters of Scottish football Rangers are hated. Outwith the religious aspect and its obvious undertones, I am still amazed at how some players and some teams get so worked up when they face the Rangers.

People are jealous of our size, our resources and our potential. That jealousy can lead to resentment and, in some cases, hate. Okay, I'm biased but you are not telling me that your average team is as keen to beat Dundee United, Aberdeen or even Celtic as they are to put one over on Rangers. I think we are thought of as a bit flash and the world wants to cut us down to size, and I was never more conscious of that than in the first season of the Souness regime.

All the big name arrivals made us the targets for Scottish football and we were made well aware of it time and time again. But that hostility worked in our favour. It totally united the squad in a them–against–us way. We *had* to stick together as a team – that was obvious – and the dressing-room atmosphere was quite simply superb. There was no one in that squad that I couldn't share a couple of beers with. The big name boys and the lads who had come up through the ranks mixed together perfectly.

The Scotland-England camps, rather than being divisive, were great for morale. We had Scotland v England five-a-sides, snooker games and quizzes. To help the numbers some days I was even made an honorary Englishman because, as big Butch put it, I'd spent some time with Sunderland reserves. Then Avi Cohen and Jimmy Nicholl arrived, and we had a United Nations select.

The longer the season went on the stronger our morale grew. We were a team – in the true sense of the word.

It took a while to recover from that bad start to the League, but by the end of the year we were firing on all cylinders. By then Graham Roberts had joined us from Spurs – striking up an instant rapport with the Rangers fans and forming a magnificent central defensive partnership with Terry Butcher. As we won seven games in a row, Celtic hit a slump and suddenly we were top of the League and looking good.

But not that good. On 31 January, lowly Hamilton came to Ibrox on Scottish Cup business and beat us 1-0. It was the first goal Chris Woods had conceded to a Scottish club since the previous November. We had been playing so well, looking so confident. It was a real stunner.

Don't ask me how it happened. I still haven't worked it out. It was just one of those days that make football the game it is. Every one of their men played out of his skin, while the majority of us had an off day. They defended brilliantly and took the one chance that came their way. We just never got going. Unlike that horrendous Cup defeat by Dundee a couple of seasons earlier, I hadn't had a lot of chances to miss. Dave McKellar, in their goal, had one superb save off me in the first half, but apart from that they contained us very well.

The papers tore us apart, and I was furious at one which forged a link between this latest setback and Rangers Cup defeat in Berwick in 1967. It was pointed out that after Berwick, Rangers two main strikers, Forrest and McLean, had never played for the club again. Would the same fate befall two strikers with the same initials, Fleck and McCoist? Of all the things that have been written about me, and there has been plenty of stick, nothing has angered me as much as that. But, fortunately, the manager treated that drivel with the contempt it deserved and ignored it.

But what couldn't be ignored was the fact that now we were out of the Cup. The League just had to be won. Our noses were in front. They had to stay there.

As the title race entered the final straight the pressure on the team was quite unbelievable. We were leading but couldn't afford any slip-ups. All the players could sense how much the fans wanted the League title. Important goals weren't so much greeted by roars of elation, more gasps of relief.

I remember we played Motherwell at Ibrox at the end of March. They defended brilliantly against us and as the match entered its final minute, it looked as if we had dropped a big point. That wouldn't have been just a blow to us, but a big psychological boost to our nearest rivals Celtic, whom we were due to play the following week at Parkhead.

But another marvellous aspect of that team was that we didn't know how to give up. In the closing seconds we forced another corner and as the ball came into the goalmouth it sparked a huge mêlée. The ball seemed to bob around the Motherwell six-yard box for an eternity and I'm sure everyone of our team – except Chris Woods – was in there trying to force the ball over the line. Eventually it spun to me and I helped it to squirm over the line from about 18 inches out. Honestly, I'm lethal from that range.

It wasn't the prettiest goal I ever scored. It certainly wasn't the hardest, but it was one of the most important. Two more points. Another big leap towards the title. I celebrated that one in style and so did the rest of my team-mates and the punters.

But the one I felt the Rangers fans really did enjoy was a Wednesday night midweek match with Dundee at Ibrox in mid-April. We pounded them from the first minute, but could we get that final lethal touch? No. As the match went on, so our pressure increased, but our luck didn't change. We still couldn't find a way through, and time was running out.

The fans were brilliant. They were totally committed to our cause. If we made mistakes then they voiced their disappointment not their anger, and that atmosphere helped the players keep their cool and not start to panic. Eventually we cracked it, Davie Cooper scoring a good goal. In typical McCoist style, I nearly messed it up by sprawling in an offside position right on the goal line, but I managed to fall *into* the actual goal area, so I wasn't offside.

You could actually feel the relief and the release of tension all round the stadium when Coop's effort hit the net. The fans wanted that title badly . . . and it showed. Thankfully, I added another soon after and that 2-0 victory took us another step nearer.

But all the celebrations that night fade into insignificance when I begin to compare them to the memorable day at Pittodrie at the beginning of May. We never expected to clinch the title that afternoon. On the contrary, it was meant to be a really difficult day for us when our nearest rivals Celtic were expected to close the gap. They were playing lowly Falkirk at Parkhead and were odds on to grab the two points, improve their goal difference and take the title race to the final game of the season the following Saturday. In comparison our record at Pittodrie suggested that we were in for a tough time and we would do well to maintain our slim advantage at the top of the table.

But you know what they say? It's a funny old game . . . and so it proved.

For a start we got off to a flier, big Butch scoring with a magnificent header after only five minutes. I can still remember the feeling of elation as I chased the big fellow and jumped on his back. What a moment!

Not that it was all plain sailing that day. We had the manager sent off and had more than a few anxious moments after Aberdeen equalised. But in the end we were well worth our 1-1 draw.

Of course as the match drew to a close we could tell from our punters' reactions that Celtic were in trouble. And so they were. They had lost 2-1, so when the final whistle blew the Pittodrie point meant we had won the title. It was official. No one could catch us. There were no ifs, buts or maybes about it. We were the Champions.

My first feeling was one of pure, undiluted joy followed quite rapidly by fear. Our punters poured on to the park and went overboard with their congratulations. I had my jersey, my left boot and my gold neckchain ripped from me as the troops swooped on me for souvenirs. There were so many people patting me on the back that I could hardly get a breath. It was really quite scary. But order was quickly restored and we retreated to our dressing-room while the police cleared the pitch to allow us a proper lap of honour.

There were great scenes on the park and afterwards in the dressing-room. All the players were congratulating one another.

The manager and the chairman made quick speeches thanking us all for our efforts. Only one thing was missing. Where was the champagne? We had been so sure that the race for the League championship would go to the final day that we hadn't even packed the champers when we headed for Pittodrie. Don't tell me it was going to be a dry run home back to Glasgow. Thankfully, we resolved that problem by stopping at an Aberdeen hotel to load on supplies, then it was back on the road to Glasgow for the best journey I've ever had in my life.

I heard some people say that they wished we'd clinched the title at Ibrox. I disagree. I wouldn't have swopped that bus journey back for anything. No one could sit still in their seat for any length of time. We all wanted to be up and about, talking to one another – laughing and joking. League Champions – what a feeling!

Everyone was on a huge adrenalin high. We didn't really need the champagne but we enjoyed it anyway! In fact we even gave some away. I passed a bottle out of the window to a delighted bus full of Rangers fans who stopped beside us on the run down the road. They couldn't believe their luck.

Unlike previous cup finals, there was no celebration party back at Ibrox, but it didn't matter. The lads went their own way and had their own party. Jimmy Nicholl and I finished back in East Kilbride. Don't ask when or how we got to our beds. We were real stretcher cases. It was one of those nights.

The only cloud on an otherwise brilliant day was the loss of my neckchain. It was a good one . . . and it really meant a lot to me. But I was to strike lucky there too. Two days after the match my father got a strange phone call from a woman asking if he was in fact the father of Ally McCoist. He said yes, but the woman was quite insistent. Could he prove he was my father? After a bit of banter he eventually convinced her that I was his son and what could he do to help her? She explained that she thought she had some property that belonged to me and wanted to return it. She asked for my dad's address and a recorded delivery parcel arrived soon after.

It was my gold neckchain – but no clue as to where it had come from. I can only guess it was the very angry mother of the guy who had grabbed it off me on the pitch and I can't thank her enough for her honesty.

And so the chain was back in place for the final game of the season against St Mirren. What a strange experience that match was. A full house at Ibrox but no pressure on us at all. Particularly when Robert Fleck scored a superb goal to give us an early lead. We never lost that advantage and the match ended as it began with the massed Ibrox choirs giving full voice to the 'Championese' song. What a great feeling! All the bad times in the past didn't matter. This was worth the agony.

I thought of the season just finished – how Graeme Souness had earned my respect and I felt sure I'd earned something in his eyes too. I listened to the cheers and thought of the superb players who had worn the Rangers jersey with distinction in previous years yet never won a League medal. And I realised how grateful I was that I wasn't to be one of them.

Nothing can beat that winning feeling.

Chapter Ten

THE GOOD, THE BAD AND THE NASTY

THAT magical day at Pittodrie was the start of a fantastic run for Rangers. We were to win the Championship four more times in the next five years; there were League Cup successes and the club itself got bigger and bigger.

On a personal note, my career had continued to soar too. I was scoring goals regularly for the team, and had become an accepted member of the Scotland squad. I had a great rapport with the Ibrox fans, who seemed to have forgotten their first opinions of me. In the middle of my contract, which still had two years to run, Rangers had offered me a new five-year deal with marvellous terms which I'd been delighted to sign.

A new owner, David Murray, had control of the club and he was making it even bigger and better, with money being spent on making the stadium even grander and attracting some of the top names in Europe to help fill it.

Life in the McCoist garden should have been rosy, but there was one cloud on my horizon, a small cloud at first but one which eventually was to overshadow everything – my relationship with Graeme Souness.

Let me stress straight away that the arrival of Souness was instrumental in taking Rangers to where they are today. He was the big name who lured the equally big names to come to Scotland. It wasn't too many years ago that we were getting the 8,000 crowds at Ibrox, and League titles were a faint hope by early March. Souness sparked a remarkable turnaround in a relatively short time.

And the arrival of Graeme Souness was also a vital step in the making of Ally McCoist, footballer. If Jock Wallace was the manager who saved my career, then Souness was undoubtedly the man who refined my game and made me as near to the finished article as I'd ever be.

The best thing he did for me was to bring himself to my career at a time when my game and confidence were sky high and I was ready for improvement. And improve it he did simply by doing the things that came naturally to a great player. I was accomplishing feats on the park that I just would not have been trying had he not been there.

He was an absolute dream to play with. I still miss him on the park now. He had great vision and brought a new dimension to our play as a team and my own game as an individual. There is still nobody in Scotland who can hit an early pass like he could. Paul McStay, on his day, can come close and Derek Ferguson occasionally, but it was a consistent and regular part of the Souness game – and I loved it.

When he had the ball in midfield, I used to try and look totally disinterested in proceedings, as if I was expecting him to pass square. Then 'bang', I'd go off on a run, relying on a bit of pace to get me clear and, nine times out of ten, Souness would spot it and hit me with the perfect pass. It wasn't anything we rehearsed. It was just the natural thing for a great player like him to anticipate and execute.

You'll never hear a bad word from me about Graeme Souness the player. And strangely, if we had been straightforward team-mates, I think we'd have got on really well. From what I've heard of his playing days at Liverpool, he liked a laugh as much as anyone. But obviously, as manager, he felt he had to stand aloof from most of the dressing-room nonsense, and we didn't get the chance to strike up the kind of rapport that team-mates generally do.

Looking back, I think he might agree with me that playing and managing Rangers at the same time worked to his disadvantage.

Playing for Rangers brings its own pressures that only those who have experienced them can imagine. Look at the big name players through the years who have come to Ibrox and struggled initially – no matter where they have come from. People usually take time to settle into a new place, and you generally don't get the time at Ibrox. It's pressure from the word 'go'.

So Souness had that to cope with – and he was also managing the club. Now that alone must be one of the toughest jobs in football. I think he took some of the pressures as a manager on to the park with him, instead of just the pressures as a player, and it showed in his disciplinary record up here. Although he had a reputation as a hard, tough competitor down south, he had far more problems with referees up here, and that just proves to me that mixing the two jobs didn't work.

I've thought long and hard about why things went wrong with us. There was no particular incident, just a gradual feeling that I was taking more than my fair share of stick in dressing-room post-mortems. I was forever being compared unfavourably to Ian Rush. I don't think he ever forgave me for not being a Rushie clone. I was told I wasn't as mentally alert as Rush. I didn't work as hard as him. I didn't finish as well as him, and so on and so on.

Now I'm not saying I didn't deserve some verbals. I remember being told by Souness one day that I wasn't doing enough work and thinking how unfair it was when I flashed back in time and remembered Archie Robertson telling me as a schoolboy that I only ever did enough to get by – no more than was necessary. So that criticism got to me, and I started trying to work for the entire 90 minutes. Always keeping on the move, trying to keep defenders as busy when I didn't have the ball as when I did.

But I didn't do that to please Graeme Souness. I worked harder for myself to make me a better player. There's a difference.

So there was friction between us, perhaps not right at the start, but certainly fairly early into our relationship. Looking back, I was probably my own worst enemy. Others would take a tongue-lashing in silence, I would answer back.

Sometimes I was just plain stupid, like after the 1987-88 New Year's Day game against Celtic at Parkhead. We lost 2-0 but we were fortunate to escape with that. It was a shocking performance. I hadn't played well. The team hadn't played well and Souness was not a happy man. I was soon receiving the sharp end of his tongue.

'You were our worst man out there,' he barked at me.

'No I wasn't,' I hit back. 'You were.'

Well, I've never seen him so angry, and he had every right to be. I shouldn't have said that. I was so sick at the way the game had gone that I just couldn't bite my tongue. Across the dressing-room I could see Ian Durrant shaking his head in disbelief as if to say, 'What have you done, Coisty?' But by then it was too late.

The manager and Wattie Smith tore my game to shreds, and I was left to reflect that sometimes silence is golden. Unfortunately, the message didn't sink in. I had this ability to annoy him when he didn't want to be annoyed.

A perfect example of that came a few seasons back when I arrived a fraction late for training to find all the lads and the managerial team gathered in the dressing-room to be spoken to by the club doctor, Donald Cruickshank. Strict new rules on medication were being introduced on FIFA's orders and all the players had to know what was happening.

My late arrival had not pleased the manager.

'Any time you're ready, Ally, we'll carry on,' he said sarcastically.

Well, I was busy getting changed while the doc warned the squad that even totally innocent cold cures like Lemsip were liable to contain banned drugs and we had to consult with the club before taking anything. Then Graeme Souness reminded us to be careful when we were out in case some troublemaker tried to spike our food or drinks with a banned substance. He then went on to tell us how when he and Trevor Francis were playing in Italy, Trevor went down with food poisoning on the eve of a big game because someone had tampered with his meal in a restaurant.

'Can you believe that?' asked the manager. 'They spiked Trevor's chicken.'

Then I piped up from outside the circle where I was just finishing getting stripped: 'Well, boss, the Italians are famous for that.'

Celebration time! The ball's in the net and I'm off and running.
(Daily Record)

Building sandcastles at Millport, age three. Get a load of that blond hair.

Here I am, age six (third along), wearing the Rangers strip I won in a local newspaper competition.

My mum told me to get a haircut for my school photo . . . I didn't listen.

John Cook of Sunderland, George Best and a young Alistair McCoist.

It's an honour to meet you. Margaret Thatcher, then Prime Minister, looks quite overwhelmed in my company. (Daily Record)

Mr and Mrs. A kiss for Allison on our wedding day – without doubt the best day of my life. (Daily Record)

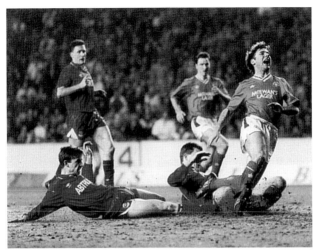

Ouch! It's not all fun and games. A painful moment as I try to escape from the Aberdeen defence. (Daily Record)

Head boy. There are not too many of them, so I can enjoy this header against Falkirk. (Daily Record)

Soulmates. Ian Durrant and I.

Strike two. Mo Johnston and I were partners for Scotland – on and off the park. (Daily Record)

Aerial combat with my big buddy Dave Macpherson, now back at Ibrox. (Daily Record)

Relaxing with a beer . . . but never before a game.

'Famous for what?' snapped Souness, still not pleased with me.

'Fowl play,' I replied, and the dressing-room erupted into gales of laughter.

The manager tried hard to restore order, but it was a lost cause. I could see him glaring at me, obviously annoyed that I had ended a serious discussion on a flippant note.

But I think that is one of the areas where he went wrong. I'm sure he wanted to join in the laughter, but felt he couldn't – that his authority had been challenged. But it hadn't.

It is very strange but although part of him disliked me for being a smart ass – always too quick with the clever answer – I'm sure part of him liked and respected me for standing up to him. I have a sneaking feeling that the only people he does respect are those who don't back down to him – and there were not too many of them at Ibrox.

When things were getting to me, and believe me they really did at times, I became more and more determined not to let him see how I was really feeling. I laughed louder, joked more often, smiled even wider, to try to let him think I didn't care. It sounds silly, but it was important to me.

Sometimes he enjoyed the joke, too. We were climbing on board the team bus one day and the manager was reading a newspaper linking me with yet another transfer move – this time to Aberdeen.

'Looks like you're on the move again, Coisty,' he says, pointing to the headline. 'That's good money Aberdeen are offering.'

Whether he meant it or not, I'll never know. I just scoffed, and said, 'Don't be silly, boss, you'd never sell me. Who'd get your goals?'

I could hear his chuckles as I walked up the bus, and never heard another word about it.

It is just a fact of life that for virtually the entire Souness reign at Ibrox, I was constantly linked to transfers. Even when I was signing new contracts, scoring goals regularly and never out the team, there always seemed to be some whisper about a possible move here or there appearing in print. Although Souness occasionally issued a denial, I felt he was quite happy with the speculation. Perhaps it was part of his philosophy to help keep me on my toes.

Anyway. I have the feeling that had a good offer come in for me, he might have sold me. I have absolutely no doubt that he would have sold me in season 1990-91 when the Hateley-Johnston partnership was going so well.

No, that's not right. I have no doubt he would have tried to sell me. Whether I'd have gone or not would have been another matter. If so, it would have been on my terms.

One of the saddest aspects of the Souness era was the undignified way some of the big signings left the club. The Graham Roberts situation when he was sent up to the Highlands with the third team and then made to sit on the bench was disgraceful. Despite all the rumours about dressing-room punch-ups, there was never anything remotely like that between Roberts and the manager. Yes, they had a disagreement after we lost at home to Aberdeen, but compared to some of the bawling and shouting that goes on, voices were hardly raised.

Eventually, Roberts said, 'If that's what you think of me, sell me.'

Souness replied: 'Consider yourself sold.' And eventually he was, but only after a nasty, unsavoury episode that left a sour taste in the mouth. I don't think you treat people like that.

But this was the Souness wall again. He had been publicly challenged and he had to be seen to win. I know managers have to be tough, but this was unnecessarily severe.

Terry Butcher's departure also saddened me. As I mentioned earlier, I cannot stress how important Terry was to the Rangers revival. He was much more than just a brilliant defender. He was our captain, our leader on and off the field, and someone every player respected. I saw the big fellow moments after Souness told him he was dropped for the 1990 League Cup semi-final against Aberdeen. The big man was in tears – and it was like a slap in the face to see that colossus crying.

Now, I know the manager had every right to drop a player who he thought wasn't playing well. But it could have been done in a different way to save the big man's dignity. He was due that.

There is no doubt that had the manager wanted to sell me and I didn't want to go, I would have been in for some of the

Roberts/Butcher treatment. I was prepared for the worst, but it never happened. And at no time did I ever contemplate asking for a transfer. I had a good contract, I was happy with Rangers and I had every confidence in my ability to ride out the storms.

Not that it was easy sometimes. As our relationship soured some of the rollickings I got were savage. After a game at Tannadice, I got a dreadful roasting. He came straight into the dressing-room at the end of the game and slaughtered me.

'You were a dud at St Johnstone,' he shouted. 'You were a dud at Sunderland, and you're still a ––––––– dud.'

I was stunned, and in my infinite wisdom and superb vocabulary hit him back with the immaculate line: 'Naw, I'm no.' It was all I could think of to say.

Now there was nothing constructive about that criticism. That was personal, and it hurt. Of course, my wee mate Durrant promptly nicknamed me Dudley, and the name stuck for months.

In those days when the stick was flying, there were three players who, to my mind, seemed to get more than their fair share – Stuart Munro, Ian Durrant and Ally McCoist. Of course, we had something in common – we hadn't been signed by Souness. There is no doubt in my mind that he wanted to build his own side – one that was 100 per cent Souness and although everyone got their rollickings we definitely got more than the others.

Durranty was so exceptional that I don't think even Graeme Souness would ever have seriously considered selling him, but I always felt Stuart Munro and I had to keep battling away under far more of a threat than some of the others.

Unless they are injured, no player ever wants to be substituted. And even if they are injured no player wants to be substituted towards the end of games that clinch League titles. Yet this happened to me. Despite being fully fit, more often than not, I was hooked off the field minutes before the celebrations started. And who'd be off with me? Stuart Munro. Wee things like that really got to me. I couldn't help but think they were deliberate.

There were other major snubs. I slept in for training one day, and was 20 minutes late. Now, I'm the first to admit I'm not a good time-keeper, and I'd rightly been given a few roastings for that. But I had never slept in before. The manager, however, totally over-reacted and banned me from attending a Scotland get-together – a public humiliation.

Now, I was wrong, no if, buts or maybes about that. I don't think I deserved that kind of punishment, however. And to prove my point, a few days earlier another player had also slept in, and had nothing said to him. No wonder I thought there was one law for me, another set of rules for others.

There is no doubt my commitment to Scotland annoyed the manager. He definitely tried to sway me away from the national squad. I'd come back from an international where I'd played well on the Wednesday and find myself dropped for our game on the Saturday. He reasoned that I'd left my legs in the country in midweek.

There was no subtlety about his methods. 'I don't want you to go with Scotland next week,' he'd say to me on a Saturday. We'd argue about it, and generally I'd go.

To be fair to him, I sympathise with the position he found himself in. His job was to do the best for Rangers, and he reckoned that having his men going through extra games did the club no favours. A successful Scotland wouldn't have saved his neck had Rangers been struggling.

It was a real dilemma for me because I was well aware of the fact that Rangers paid my wages and had every right to claim my first loyalty. But I enjoyed the Scotland squad and I think Rangers benefited in the long term because international football taught me some important lessons and helped my overall play and confidence in domestic competitions. But it was yet another source of friction with the manager and one that I could have done without.

Ironically, it was through international football that I found out about the biggest challenge I was about to face at Ibrox, and also learned another example of Graeme Souness's nastiness.

Both of us were in Italy for the 1990 finals, Souness watching the action, me a very disappointed squad member after being left out the starting line-ups for the opening two games. After those two matches Souness met a friend of mine, and the conversation switched to my non-participation in the opening games.

'Ally will be disappointed at not playing,' my friend said to Souness.

'He'll be even more disappointed when he finds out who I've just signed – Mark Hateley,' said Souness.

I think that was a really cheap jibe. Did he not care that his remark would get back to me? Did he hope it would? Either way, it was the last thing I wanted to hear as I tried to lift myself from the disappointment of Italy.

There was obviously no doubt in his mind which of his two strikers – McCoist or Johnston – was under threat. It was yours truly. Mo Johnston had had a fantastic first season as a Rangers player. I had scored more goals, but Mo had been quite sensational. There was no way Souness was going to drop him.

He had been after Hateley for some time now, and obviously was going to give him every chance, so it looked like I had a real fight on my hands to keep my place.

Sure enough, pre-season training and warm-up games saw me third choice striker. And the writing was on the wall when I was picked in midfield for the opening game of the season – a friendly against a razor-sharp Dynamo Kiev who thumped us 3–0.

Big Mark, struggling to get match sharp, took some stick from the Ibrox punters, but the manager wasn't for changing anything and I had to wait. I spoke to Souness about the situation, and he was quite blunt. He said that no one, not even me, had a divine right to keep his place in the team, and I had to agree with that. I knew then that I had to keep playing away, in midfield or not, and try to get as many goals as possible.

It looked good when I scored three from midfield in an early match with Raith Rovers. But that only delayed the inevitable. Soon the manager had the midfield he wanted, and I wasn't one of them. On to the substitutes' bench I went.

It wasn't easy. When you have been a first team regular for a number of seasons, it is a real slap in the face to be told you are not that vital any more.

Looking back to that 1990–91 season, I owe the Rangers fans a huge thank you. It was them that kept me going when I was at my lowest. They chanted my name when I warmed up, cheered whenever I came on. They were just brilliant.

It was not as if the team were struggling. On the contrary, they were playing well, and Mo and Mark were combining as if they were made for each other. My argument was that the club would be doing just as well with me in the team, but I couldn't prove that from the bench.

But still the fans chanted my name. In a sense they were so good to me that they might have done me a disservice as far as the manager was concerned. He was a man who didn't like being told what to do. And there were 30,000 voices giving him their advice. No way was he going to be told by them.

So on I struggled, getting the odd appearance here and there – scoring the occasional goal and waiting for my big chance. But even when the big opportunity came, and I seized it, it didn't seem to do me any good.

The Aberdeen game at Ibrox will live with me till I'm 100. They came to Ibrox as our nearest title challengers – it was a big, big game for us. But Trevor Steven was injured and I came on. The atmosphere was incredible – a full-house Ibrox, the game poised to go either way.

And then I scored one of the best goals I've ever notched for the club. I took a ball with my back to the Aberdeen goal, flipped it over the defender marking me, and volleyed it high into the net. Well, I went berserk. I gave it the robotic dance routine, the punters went wild as every Rangers man in the place celebrated. Well, nearly everyone. Graeme Souness, watching in the stand, didn't move a muscle.

I found out later from a number of people that the manager, never usually slow to celebrate a goal, didn't even crack a smile. Why?

We were to find out on Monday. I scored another incidentally, but Aberdeen came back to snatch a 2-2 draw, and that led to an in-depth post-mortem at the start of the following week. Souness was berating our performance. 'You were all dreadful against Aberdeen – a shocking display,' he says, and looks at me. 'Even when you scored that goal, I couldn't force myself to cheer, I was so down at the way the team was playing.'

I could hardly believe what I was hearing. That was a good goal, a vital goal, and although we let Aberdeen off the hook later on, that shouldn't have stopped him enjoying the moment of the strike. What did I have to do to please the man? I was really down, and convinced now that whatever defect Souness found in my personality was affecting his assessment of me as a player.

Super goal or not, I was back on the bench, and although I was trying to put a brave face on it, it was getting to me, boy, was it getting to me.

Eventually, I cracked, when I least expected myself to. Prior to a Cup-tie, the lads went for a short break to St Andrews – some rest and relaxation before a big game. Graeme Souness wasn't even there. But all of a sudden, I just felt out of it. We were sitting in a pub, having a few beers, laughing and joking as usual, with one exception – me. I found myself looking at my team-mates, and asking myself: 'Why are you here? What have you got to laugh and joke about, you're having a rotten season?' Suddenly I couldn't keep up the pretence any more. I had nothing to contribute. I was off.

I went back to our hotel and asked the receptionist to phone me a taxi to take me back to East Kilbride. I went upstairs to pack. There was a knock at the room door, and in came Walter Smith, presumably alerted by reception.

'Where are you going?' he asked me.

'I'm going home, Walter,' I said. 'I don't feel good. I don't want to sit and have a laugh. There's a reserve game tomorrow night, and I want to play in that. So I'll just go home now.'

Walter looked at me, realised my determination and said, 'It's up to yourself, then,' and I went downstairs.

I was in a foul mood. I gave the receptionist an absolute mouthful for telling Wattie about my taxi order, saying it was my business and no one else's if I wanted a taxi. I jumped into the taxi and told the driver, 'Look mate, I know you're probably a Rangers fan, and a great guy, but please do me a favour and don't talk to me. If I fall asleep, just wake me up in East Kilbride.'

He did as I asked, and I sat and simmered all the way home.

Why had I cracked there and then? Was it because Souness wasn't there? Had the manager been at St Andrews maybe I'd have kept up the act of laughing indifference.

I presume Walter told him about my departure, but I'll never know. It was never mentioned again. Life went back to normal for me, back on the bench, but the outburst seemed to have helped release some of the then tension inside me. I could cope,

I decided, with whatever was in store for me. Nothing would ever rattle me as much again.

I was about to be proved completely wrong.

Chapter Eleven

A DAY AT THE RACES

WHEN I was at my lowest during that miserable 1990-91 season, a lot of people worked hard to keep my spirits up. Family, friends, team-mates, Rangers fans all played their part in lifting me. But it's ironic that at the moment I came nearest to walking out on Rangers and Souness, it was one of Celtic's famous Lisbon Lions who advised me to stop and think again.

The whole sorry episode had started with my infamous visit to Cheltenham racecourse for their National Hunt Festival. Even today, if I go to any race track, some punters will shout, 'Hey, are you meant to be here, Ally?' It's funny now, but it wasn't then.

In March we were due to play Celtic in a Cup-tie, which had been switched to the Sunday for live TV purposes. This meant that we had a couple of days off in midweek, the Wednesday and Thursday. After training on Tuesday morning, the manager told us he'd see us on Friday morning and that with the big Cup-tie coming up on the Sunday, we should relax for a couple of days.

Well, that suited me perfectly. Different people do different things to relax. I like going racing. Since my Sunderland days, I've found a visit to a racecourse the perfect way to unwind, and for the previous two years had managed down to catch some of the Cheltenham action. This couldn't be better.

So early on Tuesday afternoon, I drove down with a couple of mates. We went to the races on the Wednesday, the middle day of the meeting. Back to Cheltenham on the Thursday, but this time only for part of the card. I stayed and watched the big race of the meeting, the Gold Cup, and left straight afterwards.

Even then I was conscious of not being late back on Thursday, so although I could get a lift right back home which would get me in at midnight, I asked for a drop at Birmingham Airport, to catch a flight north. I was home in East Kilbride in a couple of hours. Incidentally, I've got the perfect witness to back all this up – the chairman's brother was on the same flight.

Back at training on the Friday, the manager was relaxed and chatty. 'Did you do your Cheltenham thing this year, Ally?' he asked me, and smiled when I confirmed it. Nothing was said then. Surely if I had stepped out of line, that was when I should have got my bollocking?

And another thing, I heard in the dressing-room that four of my team-mates, who have to remain nameless, had played golf on the Thursday. Now golf was banned, on the manager's orders, but racing was not. But once again, nothing was said.

The first indication that there was anything wrong came at Parkhead on the Sunday. I wasn't in the team. That was a blow because I've got a good record against Celtic, and part of me was hoping he might have found a slot for me even playing just off the front two.

But there was worse to come. I was not even on the substitutes' bench, and no explanation why.

Well, I was absolutely livid. I walked out of the dressing-room without saying a word and stormed into the Parkhead players' lounge in a rage. I was just about ready to jack it all in. No way was I going to watch the game.

I was getting ready to phone for a mate to come and collect me, when Celtic backroom man Bobby Lennox walked in. He could sense my anger.

'Are you not playing?' he asked me.

'No, not even sub,' I replied. 'And I'm not staying for the game.'

Bobby, a Lisbon Lion in 1967, was superb. 'Ally, don't do that,' he warned me. 'Can't you see it is just what your manager wants you to do? Don't play into his hands.'

Looking back, it is one of the best pieces of advice I've ever been given. If I stormed out then, it would have been public knowledge, words would have been said, and my Rangers career might have ended that afternoon.

As it was the story was far from over.

Rangers had a dreadful afternoon. We lost the Cup-tie 2-0, but worse, lost all composure on the park and had Mark Walters, Terry Hurlock and Mark Hateley sent off and Trevor Steven carried off with a bad knee injury.

I sat in a rage in the dug-out and saw all this unfold. In fact, I could hardly bear to watch the action.

When Trevor was injured I went into the dressing room with him. He was in real pain, but the medical diagnosis was that there was no lasting damage.

With the match going out live on TV, Trevor's wife would have seen him taken off and I told Trevor I'd phone her and tell her the injury wasn't too serious.

I made the call, and she was pleased to hear the news. As I walked back through the dressing room to go back out to the pitch, Trevor, grimacing with pain, asked me: 'What did the missus say then?'

'She said she can't believe I'm not playing,' I answered, still trying to be the joker, even in moments of deepest gloom.

And gloom there was. Although the manager didn't say anything to me directly at Parkhead, the word filtered through to me that he was upset about my Cheltenham trip and that was why I wasn't sub. But was that true? Or had he already decided to drop me from the bench, and just used Cheltenham as an excuse?

Since I first kicked a ball in professional football, the punishment for everything is a fine. The theory seems to be, they are professionals, hit them where it hurts – in the pocket. So, late-keeping – a fine. Indiscipline on or off the field – a fine. Improperly dressed – a fine.

Was I fined for Cheltenham? No! At no time was any form of club discipline meted out to me. Quite honestly, I had done nothing wrong. But that wasn't to save me from another public humiliation.

On Tuesday morning, the manager spoke to me after training. He said he wanted me to talk to the press and apologise for my behaviour in going to the races the previous week. I couldn't believe my ears, and asked him to repeat it. He did, and I said that I wasn't prepared to do that. He said that if I didn't talk to the press, he would.

I decided that it might be in my own interests if I at least defended myself. My head was spinning, so I went and sat down in the toilets and tried to compose myself, thinking what I would say. Souness had wanted me to admit to an indiscipline, and say I was wrong, and I thought long and hard about how I would phrase it. Eventually I said the following: 'In the manager's opinion, there's been a breach of discipline which I have to accept.'

I tried to remain calm and dignified, and although I was shaking inside I thought I composed myself well throughout that brief meeting with the press. I desperately wanted to shout out, 'This is a disgrace', but I didn't want a public slanging match in front of the media.

Of course, the next day my 'apology' was headline news. After two days of the papers slamming Rangers' performance at Parkhead and the three orderings off, suddenly McCoist was the big story, the Parkhead on-field shambles forgotten. The idea was to try and make me the scapegoat for what had gone wrong at Parkhead. No one will ever convince me otherwise.

I like to think a lot of people saw through the Souness ploy for what it was, but some bought it hook, line and sinker. Some of the press wrote opinion pieces saying Souness was 'quite right'. I totally disagree. If I had done wrong going to Cheltenham, he would have fined me, and still played me, either from the start or on the bench. That's the way it works in football. He decided to drop me for Parkhead, then tried to make me carry the can when it went wrong. And that was hard to take.

Of course, the next day the manager spoke to me.

'Right, that's all in the past now – all forgotten about. And you'll be playing from the start at the weekend.'

We were due to face Celtic, this time in a League match. And why was I playing? Because Mark Hateley was suspended.

By this time, not only was I on an emotional low, I was struggling for fitness. For a couple of months I'd been carrying an injury and it just wouldn't clear properly. Ironically, I'd picked it up playing for Scotland against Bulgaria. At first it was diagnosed as a straightforward groin strain, and rest was reckoned to be the best cure. But as the weeks went by, it never really healed properly, and I felt a bit neglected. That is not a reflection on the Ibrox medical team, more the order of priority the manager placed on his injured players.

I felt that if I'd been one of the big name signings in the team every week, my injury would have been given a bit more attention than it got. I just feel that Souness neglected me, and I was the man who came back eight days after a knee operation and played an away leg in Europe. Where was my return for that?

Anyway, after months of trying to cure a groin injury, I eventually got to see an expert who promptly diagnosed a hernia problem and whipped me down to London for an operation. And on top of all that the team had hit a real slump. From looking as if we'd romp away with the League in early February, points had been disappearing and now Aberdeen were breathing down our necks.

Then came the bombshell. Graeme Souness was leaving us for Liverpool. I can still remember my jaw dropping in amazement when I heard the news.

My first reaction was a mixture of confusion, maybe even bitterness. As I said, we had gone off the boil. The League was to be won or lost in the next couple of weeks, and there was the manager heading off to leave us in the lurch.

I thought chairman David Murray handled the situation really well. I think he felt hurt by the whole episode, but he didn't hang about. I believe Graeme Souness wanted to stay until the end of the season, but that would have been very unsettling and it was right to get his departure over and done with as quickly as possible.

Most people expect that I must have been absolutely delighted when Souness left, but that was not really the case. I remember talking to Ian Durrant, Terry Hurlock and Richard Gough on the day he resigned. We spoke about what he had achieved at the club in his time, and that was considerable, and how he would do at Liverpool. We talked about how things would be at Ibrox in his wake.

There was no doubt his departure was going to change things for me, however slightly. But I wasn't gloating, nor was

I broken-hearted. If Graeme Souness was manager at Ibrox just now, then I don't think I would still be at Rangers Football Club. I think the gulf between us was too great by then and he had long-term plans which didn't feature Ally McCoist.

I don't feel I won, because I'm still at Ibrox and he is not. I never wanted to leave Rangers, and I nearly did because of what I think was unfair treatment of me by him. But painful and all as it was at the time, I'm not one for holding long-term grudges. We have met since and shared a few laughs. There is no animosity.

I was shocked to learn of his health problems, and I'm 100 per cent sure he has the strength of mind and body to fully recover from his triple bypass and mould the Liverpool side he wants.

Incidentally, I hear on the soccer grapevine that the Liverpool lads didn't know what hit them when he first arrived. We certainly knew what they were getting, but it was a bit of a culture shock to them.

And I hear too that their new manager was giving Ian Rush some stick for taking too long to come back from injury. And who did Graeme Souness hold up to Rushie as a shining example of a player getting back on the park in as short a time as possible? Why, that lad Ally McCoist, of course.

But while that was going on, that lad Ally McCoist had some unfinished business to attend to back in Scotland trying to help rescue a League title that was fast slipping away.

With Walter Smith now confirmed as the new manager we came to the last game of the season, and it couldn't have been more dramatic – Aberdeen, our visitors at Ibrox, only needed a point to lift the title. We had to win, but it wasn't going to be easy.

It was the walking wounded who took the field that day. John Brown played from the start with an injury and Ian Durrant and I were on the bench, both anything but 100 per cent fit – just there to fill a jersey really.

The build-up to the game had been incredible. It had been a long time since the two teams challenging for the title had met in a last game decider. The fact that we had blown such a commanding lead, the fact that Walter had just got the job. The pressure was unbelievable.

It couldn't have worked out better. Mark Hateley scored

with a superb header just before the interval to put us ahead and added another just after the break. The title was ours if we kept our cool.

Then Tommy Cowan was injured, and Durranty had to go on. He could hardly walk, never mind run, and he was in a better condition than me. But when John Brown took a knock, I had to go on. I'd like to say I contributed much, but I don't think I did. I filled a space and was nuisance value, but with a hospital operation looming, I didn't have many options.

As the final whistle neared, and I knew Aberdeen weren't going to get the two goals they needed I started to feel the whole emotion of the occasion get to me. We were going to win another title. Despite all that had happened during the season, I had played my part – not as much as I'd have liked but still a worthwhile contribution. I had earned my place in the celebrations that were about to follow.

The final whistle blew, the crowd roared in triumph, I raised my hands in thanks to the fans who had been so loyal to me throughout the season.

And I cried my eyes out.

Chapter Twelve

A DAY IN THE LIFE OF
A SCOTLAND PLAYER

A FIRM rap on the door wakes me out of a deep sleep. It is the Gleneagles porter delivering the morning newspapers as requested and the banner headlines on them are an instant reminder of the importance of the day.

It is Wednesday, 8 March, 1989, and Scotland are playing France that night in a World Cup qualifying tie at Hampden. The result of that game will go a long way to determining whether Scotland will go to the finals in Italy the following year and I am desperate to be a part of that victory push.

As my room-mate Richard Gough sleeps on, I read the papers. Virtually everyone has me in the team, but that is more than I know. There is a meeting scheduled for ten a.m. that morning and Andy Roxburgh is going to tell us the side then. The big question mark is my fitness. I have only just returned to match action after missing a huge chunk of the season with a bad hamstring injury. Ideally I could do with a couple of more games to get me at peak sharpness, but I am feeling good and think I've done well in the practice matches while the squad have been together.

After a bad Monday night, I slept well last night, and I am feeling 100 per cent. Another knock on the door wakens Goughie. It is our breakfast arriving. As usual, the maid delivering it makes a sarcastic comment about Goughie's hair – she's been insulting it every morning –

and that cheers me up no end. We watch TV, have our breakfast and talk . . . football.

We both have another go at picking the side based on what had been tried at practice games. I'm in Goughie's team, but I won't pick myself for my own team – that is just tempting fate, I think.

Then the phone rings, or should I say Goughie's phone rings. It has been a standard joke for us during the build-up that Richard is never off the phone and that any time I use it I have to ask his permission. It's like rooming with Busby!

But this time it is for either of us. It is Laura, the Ibrox secretary, checking if we'd organised things for Ian Durrant and Chris Woods, who'd called last night looking for last-minute tickets.

By now it's nine-fifty and we head down to the team meeting. It's in the Muirton room. Will that be a lucky omen for me? We meet David Speedie and Bryan Gunn in the corridor and there are a couple of nervous jokes. It's a tense time. In come Andy Roxburgh and Craig Brown. Andy starts by thanking everyone for their effort and commitment during the squad get-together. He praises the spirit and enthusiasm of the whole group and says that some are about to be disappointed when he reads out the team. But everyone should remember that it is a squad and we all have our part to play.

He starts to read out the team and suddenly I'm very nervous. I can hear my heart pounding as I listen for my name. He says 'McCoist' and I start breathing again. I'm in. What a great feeling.

No one says, 'Bad luck, mate', or anything like that to the ones who aren't in the team. As professional footballers, I know they'll all be down that they've not been included, but being professionals they also mask that disappointment well.

We watch videos of the French, particularly at free kicks and corners and Andy spends some time with Goughie and Alex McLeish on whether they want to mark their big men man-for-man or just look after their own particular zones. Both Alex and Richard say they'd prefer the zones and that's OK by Andy.

On to the practice pitch at Gleneagles where we rehearse our own free kicks and corners. We walk through the pre-arranged moves. Most of our corners will be going deep, but Andy wants me to make a near post run. That will mostly be a decoy move to take a defender away, but it might come to me and the idea is that I'll head-flick that back to one of the big men coming in at the back. I'm a bit worried about that, and given my sometimes wayward heading ability the entire nation should be a bit apprehensive too. Mo Johnston and I are given specific tasks to do if the French get free kicks near our area. Mo has to join the wall and charge the kicker, while I've to watch for any runs from the deep.

Then Mo and I spend some time together. We work out how we'll try and confuse the French at throw-ins, and how we'll react to long balls out of our defence, who will make the first runs and what we should leave to each other.

Mo, of course, knows all the French players and we are sure that we will be marked by Sonor and Silvestre, though who will pick up whom is anyone's guess. They are both hard players who like to make their presence felt and we know we'll have to look after ourselves.

We play a practice game with totally silly sides – like all the forwards against the defenders etc. And it's a great laugh. Mo and I slag each other mercilessly if either of us miss a chance. 'If that's your best we've no chance tonight,' Mo shouts at me.

'If you play like that you WILL be a hero in France,' I give him back in reply.

Back in for lunch and a great atmosphere at the table. Alex McLeish and I are great fans of the offbeat paper Viz. We are both totally into its crude, zany humour, and we sit at lunch matching every member of the squad with one of the outrageous characters in the paper. Everyone is savaged mercilessly and everyone enjoys it. The squad spirit really is something special.

We've to go for an afternoon sleep, but there is just time for Mo and I to have a final frame of snooker. We have been playing all week and he is one up in the series. He looks like winning this one, too, but goes in off the final black to lose and you can hear my shriek of delight back in Glasgow.

Back to the room and Goughie's on the phone. There's a surprise. He's chatting to Ray Wilkins for some background about French striker Xureb, whom Ray played with at Paris St Germain. Ray warns Goughie that the Frenchman has blistering pace, particularly for the first ten yards, and that he is confident and clever. All in all a tricky customer. He wishes us both all the best, then it's lights out for a couple of hours kip.

Despite the nervous tension slowly building up in me, I sleep alright, but when the alarm call wakes us up at four p.m., I'm instantly *awake and feeling a real tingle of excitement. Pre-match nerves have well and truly started.*

We get ready in our own way for the five-thirty departure. Andy Roxburgh wants the team to be as relaxed as possible before the game and doesn't insist on any dress standard. Go in what you're most comfortable in is his theory. For me, it's a collar and tie, but Goughie prefers a tracksuit, and we are ready to go in plenty of time.

Just as we are set to head downstairs, there's a knock at the door. It's my sister Alison on route from her home in nearby Auchterarder down to the game. She's just dropped in to wish me all the best and I give her tickets for herself, the rest of my family and friends. Of course, being me, there's been a ticket mix-up – I'm infamous for them – and at the last minute I've to scour round the squad looking to buy some extras. Paul McStay comes to my rescue with four.

I head down to reception with Alison to be confronted by Andy Roxburgh, pretending to be very angry.

'And who is this?' he demands. 'You know the rules about female company.'

'I'd like you to meet my sister, Alison,' I reply.

'Coisty. Not the old sister routine,' says Andy. 'I thought you could have thought of something more original than that.'

Alison blurts out that she really is my sister, and Andy bursts out laughing. He'd known all along.

On to the bus and off to Hampden. I sit at a table for four with Charlie Nicholas, Steve Nicol and Gary Gillespie. We play cards, but it's hard to concentrate with all the noise on the bus. There's a lot of good-natured banter and loud laughter – a sure sign of nervous tension. Then we get held up in horrendous traffic and the driver performs a minor miracle going in and out of traffic cones to get us back on the move. Even so, we are going to be a lot later than we thought getting to Hampden, so Craig Brown comes down the coach telling everyone their number for the night.

I'll be wearing number nine and I'm really pleased. After all, Mo has started the last three games with that jersey on his back, but he doesn't mind switching to number eleven. That's typical of him – a great bloke on and off the park.

We don't arrive at Hampden till seven-thirty and we have to go straight out to have a look at the surface. What a roar greets us as we step out of the tunnel. The ground is really filling up and the atmosphere is electric. There is about an inch of water lying on the surface, but the rain that has been beating down stops and that's something.

Back into the dressing-room to get ready and the tension continues to build. There is a new FIFA ruling that everyone must wear shin-guards, and the ones that don't normally put them on – Mo, Goughie and Paul – are not too happy about having to comply. But there's no alternative.

Most of the talking and the laughs are now loud and exaggerated. There are a lot of encouraging shouts from the noisy ones about the importance of the game and how a win will put us firmly on the road to the World Cup finals. The quiet ones like Jim Leighton and Paul McStay sit alone with their own thoughts.

Andy Roxburgh is everywhere, sometimes yelling general instructions to the whole team, other times having individual words with certain players. His message is the same. He wants passion, but controlled passion. All the traditional commitment of wearing a Scottish jersey, 100 per cent effort, but plenty of thought too. We can do it. That big crowd out there is expecting it. We mustn't let them down.

Then all the players shake hands with each other. We wish each other all the best and tell each other we can do it. We move out to the tunnel now and wait for the French to join us. As they come out I glance quickly at them to see if I can spot any fear in their eyes. But I don't see any. On the contrary, Papin is looking relaxed and laughing and I see him shake Mo's hand. I deliberately don't look at them anymore. I don't want any eye-to-eye contact in case that leads to one of them wanting to shake my hand. I don't want that at this time. Out we go to a great roar. The French must be affected by this. I think.

Since we looked at the park 30 minutes earlier the surface water had drained away and I run to help Jim Leighton with his warm-up. I hit a few at him, but as I usually do with Rangers, I put one past him into the net. It's a silly superstition, but one I always practise.

The game starts and it is Luc Sonor, pony tail and all, who is marking me. The ball goes out of play as one of the lads tries to play it through to me and the whistle goes just as I collect it. That doesn't stop Sonor, however. He whacks me on my left calf and down I go. There's less than a minute gone.

It's a sore one, but it's not going to put me out of the game. And in a strange way it might just work to our advantage. I hear Mo and big Roy complaining bitterly and when I stand up there is real anger in their eyes.

Here is instant proof that it is going to be tough and we'll have to look after ourselves and each other. And so we do. Our tackling is sharp, we are closing down quickly and the French are more than a bit rattled. That thump I took was well worth the pain. It has fired us all up.

We win a corner on the left and, as rehearsed, I make a near post run. It comes to me and I head-flick it to the back. I turn around and see Goughie being held back as he goes for it. I scream for a penalty. The referee is having none of it, however.

Then the French come back and one of their midfielders has a great shot from just outside the box. I'm right behind him and the goal, and I'm sure it's in at the left-hand post till Jim Leighton appears and makes one of the best saves I've ever seen. I still don't know how he got to it.

What an escape and we take advantage of it. The ball breaks to me just at the edge of their box and on that surface I think it's worth a shot and have a go. The ball goes straight to Mo and my first thought is that he's offside. But I see a Frenchman desperately trying to run out at the same time and Mo slots the ball home. He goes to celebrate and I chase after him. He tries to slide to his knees on the byeline, but totally messes it up and takes a nosedive into the mud. Hampden celebrates and so do the players.

But, as so often happens, losing a goal sparks the French into life and they put together a few good moves. Suddenly we are a bit jumpy and diving in at the wrong time. Then there is a great tackle from Paul McStay right in the middle of the park. That gets the crowd roaring and the team playing again. We are back in business.

A good move down the right and Mo ends up with possession at the back post. Paul and I are running into the box at full tilt, screaming for a lay-off, but by then he's committed to the shot and his effort goes just past. He apologises for not using Paul or myself and that's the matter finished. I might well have done the same thing in his position and at least he's got a shot in. That's what strikers are for, and what's more important, we're proving that this French defence is vulnerable.

Then another chance. Ian Ferguson has a shot from outside the box, but it hits me and I touch it past Silvestre in the one movement. Suddenly I'm clear in the box, fending him off and curling a left-foot shot past Bats.

It is like watching a slow-motion replay. Firstly, I think the ball is going too high and it's going to hit the bar, then I realise it is right in the postage stamp corner. A goal. I'm off to celebrate and I won't do a Mo and fall on my coupon.

But it's not to be. I look round for my team-mates and they are all static, looking at the linesman with his flag raised. Offside. Not against me, but against Mo who was doing what a striker should do and following in on Fergie's initial shot. No way was he interfering with play, but it doesn't matter. The goal won't stand. I'm sick.

Half-time and a mixed reception from Andy Roxburgh and Craig Brown. Praise for our early efforts but Andy has some sharp words for the way we played just after the goal. We must be careful of their slick one-twos and watch the runners, not just the ball.

We have a cup of tea and there are plenty of shouts of encouragement for each other. The message is simple. We can do it. Another 45 minutes like that and Italy is a giant step nearer.

What we need to kill the game is an early second-half goal and we get it. It starts with a long ball from Goughie. Sonor and I go for it. To be honest, I make a mess of my first attempt to get it, I should have got myself between him and the ball, and he takes it away to the left-back position. I'm chasing after him, angry with myself. I'm sure he's just going to thump it up the park, but I suddenly realise he is going to take a second touch and perhaps look to find another Frenchman. Perhaps he thinks I'm further away, but whatever, he taps the ball on and I nip in front of him and steal possession. I then see Steve Nicol powering up the wing and weight my pass to him so he can take it in his stride and hit an early ball in. He does just that, but from my angle I think Battiston is going to get there first. Then Mo arrives and makes a great header. Bats can't hold it and, incredibly, we're 2-0 up.

I watch Stevie and Mo celebrating behind the goal and Goughie jumps on my back. It's a fantastic moment. I wait for Mo and congratulate him, but as we jog back to the centre line for the re-start I feel my legs becoming just a touch heavy. That lack of match action, plus the heavy sodden pitch, are beginning to take their toll . . .

But the French are down and it's showing in their attitude. Sonor starts to give me a bit of lip and I'm delighted to hear it. That shows he is rattled and I can always handle the verbals on the park.

'You bad player,' he tells me in broken English.

'Me bad player, but me 2-0 up,' I reply.

He tries again. 'You no good player.'

'*Me no good player, but me going to Italy,*' I say. '*Do you want any tickets?*'

He loses the verbals and goes back to the physical. He tries to go through me, but I sense him coming and manage to avoid most of what he was trying to do to me. We still get the foul and I stand up and laugh at him. As I go past I pretend to pat him playfully on the back, but instead get a good pull at his pony-tail. He is not amused.

I chase another pass and I'm conscious of the close attention of a defender. I'm sure it's Sonor who will be out for some revenge, so I flick back my elbow in case he gets too close. I feel a terrific bang on the elbow and I'm frightened to look round. If that was Sonor's nose my elbow has just hit, it'll be spread all over his face . . .

I don't hear any complaints behind me, so I try and rub my elbow surreptitiously, so the French don't know it's sore. I glance round and see Silvestre doing the same to his elbow. Obviously we've clashed arms when we ran for that last ball. We realise we are both behaving exactly the same way and laugh. We pass each other and slap hands by way of a truce. It's a nice moment.

Then I catch sight of Brian McClair waiting to come on and I know deep down it'll be me that's to come off as my legs have been pretty tired for that last few minutes. I go to the far touchline to waste as much time as possible when the substitution is made. Well, it has been done to Scotland many times in the past – why shouldn't we use a little time-wasting when it suits us?

But although I'm prepared for it, when I see it is definitely me to come off, I'm very disappointed. It's strange, but I feel I've let everyone down by not lasting the match.

The lads are great. As I run off I hear shouts of '*Well done, Coisty*' from Big Roy and Paul. As I pass Mo, he says, '*Different class, pal.*' But all that does is make me feel worse. I suddenly want very much to be on the park and celebrating with them when the final whistle goes.

But off I go to warm congratulations from the rest of the dugout and I watch the rest of the game from there. I realise just how brilliantly Gary Gillespie is playing and watch more great saves from Jim Leighton. Everyone raves about them after the game, but I still think his first-half one was better.

And three minutes from time, there is the added bonus of seeing my room-mate for the week, Goughie, writhing about in agony after *being caught a nasty blow in what is politely termed the groin area. He is not happy with that Frenchman at all. And his anger is not helped by hearing my roars of laughter from the dugout. What a nice way to end the game.*

The final whistle goes and we, the team and the fans, can really start celebrating. As the French players troop off the park, I catch sight of Sonor and we shake hands. Then it's into our dressing-room and warm congratulations from all the players to each other. I drink three bottles of orange juice in rapid succession and lie in a bath letting the tiredness flood over me.

But despite the elation in the dressing-room, I'm still not happy with my own personal contribution. Perhaps it is just the release of hours and hours of build-up and tension, but for an hour or so after games I am often a bit moody – switching between wild exuberance and sullen gloom. This is one of these times, and while, on the surface, I'm joining in all the team hilarity, deep down I'm still annoyed at myself for not being able to finish the game. It sounds silly. Even I know it sounds silly, but I can't help myself.

I try and hide these feelings from the team, and head out from Hampden to meet my family. I have a drink with them and leave with my fiancée Allison and a couple of friends to meet up with the rest of the squad back in Glasgow city centre.

The first person I bump into there is Frank McAvennie. He congratulates me warmly on my performance and that means a lot to me because many felt that he should be wearing the Scotland number nine shirt instead of me. Frank's genuine praise, and the laughter and joking from a very happy bunch of players works its usual trick and soon my gloom phase is over and I'm back to my normal idiotic self.

Mo had left tickets for Jim Kerr and Charlie Burchell of Simple Minds and they arrive at the post-match party. I've met them before and they are good lads. Footballers and pop people have a lot in common in terms of continually being in the public eye, and we are at ease in each other's company. We are telling football stories and they are giving us tales from the world of rock. They are due to do some recording soon and invite me along to the studio. I'm really into music and can't say 'Yes' quickly enough.

And so Wednesday, 8 March, turns into 9 March and the celebrations continue. We are looking back on what has happened over the day and looking forward to what is to come.

I just have to be happy with myself. Three months ago I could hardly run because of an injury. Four hours ago, I had run and run over a heavy, difficult surface and done my bit for my country. I had earned praise from fans, friends, family and team-mates.

This is a day I'll never forget . . .

And, thinking back, the perfect accolade came from big Roy Aitken as I left the Hampden dressing-room.

'Coisty,' he shouts. 'Well done, pal, but I hope you get stuffed on Saturday.'

It's not a bad old life . . .

Chapter Thirteen

THERE'S ONLY ONE MAURICE JOHNSTON

EARLY in my Sunderland days, Allison and I travelled down to Scarborough where Scotland's semi-professional team were playing a tournament. The main reason for the journey was to see my old St Johnstone mate John Brogan who was playing for Scotland, but among the Scots lads I met that day in Yorkshire was a young striker just making his name with Partick Thistle.

His name? Maurice Johnston. And as we laughed and joked in Scarborough back in the early '80s little did I realise how dramatically our paths would cross in the future.

Let me say straight away that I think Mo Johnston the footballer is a superb player, and Mo Johnston the person is one of the most decent lads you could ever meet. I just love his attitude to life. He enjoys a laugh, but he takes his football seriously, and I would defend him to the hilt against people who say otherwise.

I think people have the wrong impression about him. He got some bad publicity in his early days with Celtic, but so did I in my initial Rangers times. I don't think there's a bad bone in his body – he's just a right good lad.

After that initial meeting we kept in touch as his travels took him to Watford, Celtic and Nantes and we were generally room-mates when we were both in the Scottish squad.

I used to suffer from his cheeky sense of humour, particularly when it came to insulting our respective goalscoring records.

Wherever he has been, he has scored a lot of goals, and that tells you what a good, consistent player he is. His spell in England with Watford was far more successful than mine with Sunderland – a fact which he reminded me of at every opportunity. In my time down south, we had actually lost 8–0 at Watford. I'm just thankful Mo wasn't playing that day although the way he keeps going on about that you would think he had been.

But though we were Scotland striking partners, I never suspected for one moment that one day we'd be Rangers team-mates – particularly when, towards the end of the 1988–89 season Celtic called a press conference to announce that Mo would be re-joining them from Nantes next season.

The first inkling of the bombshell about to hit Scottish football came in an oblique reference from Graeme Souness, the full impact of which we only realised later. We had just lost the 1989 Cup final to Celtic, a Joe Miller goal giving them a 1–0 victory, and our dressing-room was like a morgue. The manager was down too, but he said, 'Never mind, something's going to happen in the next few weeks, which will give us the last laugh.'

What did he mean? 'Who knows, and who cares?' I thought. We had just lost a Cup final.

Then, straight after the final I went off to join the Scotland squad. My room-mate at Troon was Mo Johnston and he started dropping little hints that still went over my head. I remember him saying to me one day, 'Graeme Souness has some house, hasn't he? It's brilliant inside.'

How did Mo know what the gaffer's house was like? I thought he was winding me up.

Then he told me that he was planning to join Rangers. I swear it was like being hit by a juggernaut. There were still some details to be sorted out, so he swore me to secrecy. He was just desperate to tell someone.

But the amazing thing was that although his Parkhead move had hit some snags, Celtic were still hopeful of landing him. The whole bizarre situation was best summed up by the day Billy McNeill drove down to see Mo at our Troon hotel. Mo was just about to go to speak to Billy in the foyer, when he took a phone call in our room. It was from Grame Souness.

I actually hid my head underneath a pillow. I just couldn't

believe it was happening. But happen it certainly did – a few weeks later in a signing that had enormous implications for Rangers.

By this time we were back in pre-season training and had gone over to what had become our usual sharpening-up HQ in Italy. While Mo was being introduced at an Ibrox press conference that stunned the football world, we were already in Italy, but had a fair idea of what was going on back home. We trained in the morning and came back for lunch, to be officially told that Mo Johnston had signed for Rangers and was about to join our training camp. Obviously the management wanted us, the players, to make him as welcome as possible.

We sat down at a big communal table to eat, and Mo arrived by helicopter. We were ready for him, and had set a table for one in the corner with just bread and water on it for him alone. Well, as I thought, he loved the joke and we were off and running.

Let me emphasise straight away that Mo was totally accepted by the entire Rangers squad. There were rumours circulating that, just as some Rangers supporters objected to Mo's signing, so did some of the players. Nothing could be further from the truth. Even the true blues in the team, lads like Ian Durrant and Ian Ferguson who had been life-long Rangers fans, loved him and still speak warmly of him today.

But there was no denying that his signing had sparked a storm, and the squad were warned to be on the alert for any type of protest. It got to the ridiculous stage that there was talk that some fanatic might even make an attempt on his life.

Of course, Mo and I were rooming together in Italy and once the lights went out and the shutters came down, it was pitch dark. As we went to sleep I remember saying to Mo that if some assassin did come in, I hoped he wouldn't get us mixed up.

'I'll be throwing you in front of me,' I joked.

We had a laugh, but deep down something must have registered in my subconscious, because I woke up during the night. I was half-asleep but I was sure I could hear someone in the room!

Sure enough, someone was moving about at the door. I'll never know why but for some reason I just started screaming my head off. The whole hotel must have heard me and as I screamed I fumbled about for the light switch. Clumsily I found it, flicked it on and I'll never forget what I saw. There, crouched in the doorway where I had spotted the prowling figure, was Mo. He had his hands over his head, his face buried in his knees and he was screaming like a banshee too! He had got up to go to the toilet and was on his way back when I woke up and thought it was somebody breaking in. My shrieks had terrified him, and in a panic, he had crouched down and started screaming for help too.

Looking back, it was a hilarious moment, quite brilliant, but deep down it showed the type of pressure that he was under.

Now that a few years have gone by, it's easy to forget just how volatile a situation he had got himself into. I remember when Mo signed, Graeme Souness asked me to do a TV interview, welcoming the new signing to the club and saying he had all our backing. Terry Butcher had already done one, but the manager wanted a West of Scotland player, like myself or Ian Durrant, to do a similar piece.

I refused, not because I wasn't supporting the wee man, the facts were anything but. I told the manager that I would tell Mo to his face he had my 100 per cent backing, and I'd say the same in front of the rest of the team, not that it really needed to be said, everyone knew how well we got on, but I was a bit wary about going up front like that on TV or in the press. I had heard feelings were running high back home, and I didn't want some nutter throwing a brick through my mother's window because he thought I had said the wrong thing.

My worries about doing a simple interview emphasise just how courageous a move Mo had made. I honestly think he is the only man who could have carried that off. He had the ability to shrug things off, shut his ears when he needed to.

When the transfer rumours were flying thick and fast about me, there was even one that had Celtic bidding for me. Well, there was no truth in that, but even if there had been, I wouldn't have gone. I just couldn't have faced the flak that would have been coming from both directions, nor could I have put my family through it. Let me say it again, Mo Johnston deserves a medal for what he did.

But if Mo's arrival at our training camp grabbed the headlines in 1989, it was his premature departure from the pre-season work-out in 1990 that had the press in turmoil. 'MO SENT HOME' screamed the headlines as he arrived in Scotland early from the training camp, his face showing some interesting abrasions. There was silly talk of punch-ups with the manager, but that was just nonsense. The whole incident was blown out of all proportion and I still think to this day that Mo coming home was a huge misunderstanding.

It all started when we were allowed to have a few beers after a hard day's training. Mark Hateley had just joined the club, amid widspread speculation that it was my place in the team he was earmarked for. My pal Mo decided to stick up for me.

It was a lively discussion, to say the least, but Mo wasn't having a go at Mark Hateley, it was more a dig at the Rangers management team for bringing in someone that threatened our playing relationship. He felt very strongly about us as a striking duo and was basically having a go at Souness for putting it at risk. He didn't hold back when he felt he had a point to prove.

But although the exchanges got quite heated, the night would probably have ended quite peacefully if Mo and I hadn't decided to raid Derek Ferguson and Scott Nisbet's room. We crept into their room and Mo dived on Nissy's bed only to find the big man had moved his mattress on to the floor to help his sore back. In the darkness, Mo landed on some rusty bed springs and did his looks no good whatsoever.

That was just a silly bit of horse play which had gone wrong, but allied to the earlier verbals the manager decided Mo needed a talking to.

I still maintain, Mo was never sent home. The manager said something like: 'If you don't get your act together, you can pack your bags and leave.' I didn't think he had been sent home, but when I came back from training, his stuff was gone. I kept thinking it was a joke, and he was about to leap out from under a bed at me. But no, he was off.

Press speculation was that he would never kick a ball for Rangers again, but they were way off the mark, and after a public statement of good intent, Mo was back in the Rangers fold. Perhaps it was because of the enormous courage he had shown in joining Rangers in the first place, but I felt Graeme Souness had a real respect for Mo and tolerated more from him than he did from others.

On one occasion the team were in a hotel when John Brown's baby girl was born. Bomber was in great form, buying drinks for everyone, but eventually the manager decided enough was enough and ordered everyone to their rooms.

Unknown to him, Mo and I were in a downstairs bar and didn't hear his order. However Ray Wilkins arrived and told us what the manager had said. But Mo and I reckoned that as he hadn't told us personally we would chance our arm and stay on regardless. And so we did for another ten minutes or so, until I saw the gaffer standing in the doorway glaring at us. Mo had his back to him, and I said to him, 'Whatever you do, don't look round because he's there!'

Souness, to my surprise and delight, just about-turned and left us there, but we took the hint and hightailed it back to our room. I couldn't help wondering, however, if Mo's presence had saved me a bawling out. If it had been Durrant and I would nothing have been said?

Mo was game for anything, especially if it was for a laugh. Like that incident in the hotel, he would bend the rules rather than break them if there was a bit of extra enjoyment to be had. He was never stupid, he knew where to draw the line.

He had no sooner joined Rangers in Italy than he and I sneaked out for an illegal beer one night. We had put in two hard days' training, and there was a beer festival in the nearby town. So we thought, 'One beer, we deserve that', and nipped out of the hotel and into town. Sure enough we did just have the one drink each, but in his best Italian/French Mo had asked for two 'mucho grande' beers and you wouldn't have believed the size of the glasses they came in. They were like buckets.

When I think back now, it was a risky thing to do – for me, and especially for him. What would the press have made of Rangers' most controversial signing falling foul of club discipline in his first week? But that was typical of Mo. He fancied an idea and was off and doing it without worrying about the consequences.

Of course, I wasn't always being Captain Sensible in these situations either. So Mo had a willing partner. But I have to stress it was never anything serious, just a little cheeky. Even the management team appreciated some of it.

Like the time the team were booked into a hotel over Hogmanay to help us prepare for the New Year Old Firm clash. Naturally, there was a strict alcohol ban, but, predictably, Mo and I decided we didn't want to bring in the New Year with Lucozade. We'd each brought a bottle of champagne with us to the hotel so we would toast the start of a new year in some style.

It was meant to be our secret, and I don't know how word got out, but it did. Just about 11 o'clock, Walter Smith came to our door doing a room check. He marched straight in, and without stopping walked right up to the curtains, where we'd hidden the champagne, chilling in ice buckets, naturally. He pulled back the curtains, picked up the champagne and started laughing. It was so funny the way he did it, and soon Mo and I were in stitches. We were still laughing when our champagne disappeared out of the door in Walter's grasp. But the best part of the whole incident was still to come.

Just after the bells, there was a knock at our door, and in came Walter with our champagne and three glasses – and the three of us polished it off in quick fashion.

When Mo eventually left the club for Everton last season, everyone assumed I'd be delighted. After all, he was one of the main reasons why I had such a long spell on the bench during the previous season. On the contrary, I was gutted when he left. It's a funny thing, but although we were rivals for the same position with Rangers and Scotland, we have each tried our best to help the other get back in favour when we've been out of the scheme of things.

When I couldn't get a first team place at Rangers, no-one spoke louder and more often in my defence than Mo. He was forever asking why they couldn't play me in an attacking midfield role, just behind him and Mark Hateley. It's something I think could have been tried a bit more and I know for a fact Mo spoke to Graeme Souness, Walter Smith and even David Murray about it.

Similarly, I've had my say to try and persuade Andy Roxburgh to let Mo back into the Scotland set-up. I said publicly and I still believe fervently that we as a country are not good enough to ignore a player of Mo's ability. I think it is now a personality clash between Andy Roxburgh and Mo, and I wish I could do something to bridge the gulf because, deep down, I know they have enormous respect for each other. I respect both their stances on the matter.

Mo has also taken some very unfair criticism from Rangers fans about how quickly he left the club when things started to go wrong for him. People say that I took a season on the bench and said nothing, but as soon as Mo was dropped he was off.

But that is just the nature of the man. No matter what had happened I don't think Mo would have been at Rangers for the rest of his playing career. There are club men who stay with one team for virtually their whole football life, and there are football nomads who change scene every two years. Mo was definitely one of the latter, and it worked to his advantage. Every move seemed to recharge his batteries and he was a better player for it. Going to France was certainly a superb move for him, probably the best of his career. He came back from Nantes like a different player, a great man to have up front battling with you.

As with his arrival at Rangers, I had advance notice of his impending departure from Ibrox. He admitted straight away to me that he didn't fancy a long spell on the bench, and was thinking of leaving. He told me later that there were one or two clubs interested, including Everton, so it was no surprise when he headed down to Merseyside.

Some Rangers fans nowadays are very quick to give Mo stick, and forget what he did in his time at Ibrox. Let's not forget he gave Rangers two great years. He worked like a Trojan and made an unbelievable amount of goals for me. He was a good finisher and scored some vital ones himself.

But it was his unselfish work-rate as my striking partner that will always stick in my memory. Because his arrival at Ibrox came with so much hype, he was the attacker every defender was wary of. Often, they were so busy watching him, I got a bit of extra space and time, and tried to take advantage of it. Mo also took more than his fair share of kicks and bruises in a Rangers jersey, and just got up and got on with it.

I wish him well wherever his nomadic instincts take him,

and thank him for outstanding contributions that made Rangers a better team, and me a better player.

Cheers, pal, you were great!

Chapter Fourteen

ALLY TWO CAPS

THE scene was the Ibrox dressing-room in April 1986, two days after I had made my international debut, playing in a 0-0 draw with Holland in Eindhoven. I thought I'd done pretty well, all things taken into consideration. My Rangers team-mates obviously didn't quite share that opinion.

'Here's a question for you,' big Derek Johnstone asked the dressing-room in general. 'Which Scottish footballer earned two caps in the one day?' There was a puzzled silence from all there, and the big man eventually supplied the answer. 'Ally McCoist,' said Derek. 'Against Holland on Wednesday, he got his first and his last.'

Loud guffaws all round, and for the next few weeks I was Ally Two Caps. Coping with international stardom was not going to be easy.

Even before I made the full international team, I was the subject of some cheeky taunts from Celtic fans at Parkhead. As we went into the Old Firm encounter, I had been scoring a few goals and big Jock Wallace had said to the press that he thought I was knocking on the door of the international squad. 'ALLY FOR SCOTLAND' were the headlines as the newspapers picked up Jock's theme.

Well, as luck would have it, we were well beaten by Celtic on the day. I had a stinker and the packed Celtic fans in The Jungle started chanting, 'Ally for Scotland'. I guess there was just a touch of sarcasm there.

But when the national chance came along, I took it, and despite barbed comments from alleged friends, it went fairly well. It is not easy for strikers to show up in 0–0 games, but I put a lot of effort into it, and team boss Alex Ferguson seemed pleased. One thing would have made my night – a goal, but although I had a half-chance from a Jim Bett flick near the end, it went over the bar, and I had drawn a blank.

However, I had made the squad at a vital time. Fergie was about to announce the Scotland party for the World Cup finals in Mexico, and I felt I had an outside chance. I had scored a fair number of goals for Rangers that season, and looking at possible rivals for the striking positions, I felt I had as good a claim as most of them. But I was to be disappointed – twice.

The first came when I was getting changed after training at Ibrox and was told to go up to the manager's office. As I climbed the stairs, I could hear big Jock arguing furiously with someone on the phone. I went in, and he almost threw me the phone. He wasn't pleased.

It was Alex Ferguson, who was very complimentary about what I'd done that season, and what I'd done in Holland, but no, he wasn't going to take me to Mexico. I was as disappointed as big Jock was angry, but there was one small consolation. Fergie told me that if any of his strikers dropped out, I would be going in their place. Well, that was something.

But, I hate to say, Fergie wasn't as good as his word. Prior to the squad leaving for altitude training in America, en route to Mexico, Kenny Dalglish dropped out. But before I even had time to wait for the phone to ring, Steve Archibald had been called into the party. Now that really made me mad. What a snub!

This time there was no call from Fergie to explain that manoeuvre, and that was wrong. I really felt very hurt and let down, and I think to this day I would have done as well as any one of the front men who did make the trip. Remember, Scotland only scored one goal in three games over there, and that came from a midfield man, Gordon Strachan.

A few years passed before I got the chance to dig up Alex Ferguson about his broken promise, and in typical McCoist fashion, I made a joke of it. I was in Lilleshall for treatment and Fergie and Archie Knox came to see Norman Whiteside who was also based there. I said to Fergie: 'I bet you are still sick about not taking me to Mexico. I'm telling you, if I had gone, Scotland would have qualified.' Fergie just smiled, said nothing, and left. Oh well, some you win.

But back in Scotland in 1986, it was a very disgruntled Ally Two Caps who watched Scotland knocked out of the World Cup. Soon, however, the national scene was to change. Alex Ferguson quit the Scotland job, and was succeeded by Andy Roxburgh, with whom I'd worked at under-16 and under-18 level. Sure enough, I became a regular in Andy's squads and Ally Two Caps was eventually left behind.

Playing for Scotland was everything I expected it to be and more. It's every schoolboy's fantasy to turn out for their country, and I think the ultimate dream of every youngster is to pull on the Scotland number nine jersey. Now I was actually doing that. It felt great.

I was a real Scotland fan as a youngster. Like the rest of the country in 1978, Ally MacLeod had me convinced that we would win the World Cup. I can still remember the passion of those times. I'd stood on the Hampden terracings and cheered and suffered. I'd done the Wembley trip with my mates. I was as dedicated a Scotland fan as there was.

The Scotland squad atmosphere was superb. I have heard through the grapevine that some national squads in past years have not exactly been Scotland United. Stories of cliques and prima donna attitudes from certain players have evidently not been uncommon before. But not in my time, and the credit for that is due 100 per cent to Andy Roxburgh. He knew exactly the type of atmosphere he wanted and the type of players who would help him achieve it.

I think it is a real tragedy that the crazy demands of 44-game leagues and the like have meant he can't have get-togethers as much as he would like, because they are ideal for building morale and understanding.

The perfect example of that came when there was a weekend Scotland get-together not long after the Skol Cup final of 1989. Aberdeen were leading 1-0 in that game, when Willie Miller fouled me, and the referee gave a penalty – quite rightly, I say, but you know my opinion on all penalties I get. Some, however, didn't see it that way. Some in fact think it was one of the softest penalties ever awarded in the history of the game – in particular, William Miller Esq.

I don't think I've ever seen anyone as angry as he was that day on the park. He screamed at me, called me all the cheating so and sos you could ever imagine. He was literally incandescent with rage.

Willie and Terry Butcher were good pals, and the Dons' man even shouted at big Terry about me. 'What are you going to do about him?' he bawls at Terry. 'He's a disgrace to the game.' As if Butch was going to ask the referee to change his mind!

Of course, I didn't help the situation by patting Willie on the head and saying, 'Willie, it was a penalty. Watch it on the telly when you get home.'

If looks could have killed, I'd have been a goner, and when Mark Walters converted the spot-kick I thought Willie was going to explode. Even big Alex McLeish, who is a real mate of mine off the field, was raging at me. And although Aberdeen eventually had the last laugh by winning the Cup 2–1, there was still some resentment about the whole penalty incident.

Rather than let it simmer away quietly, Andy Roxburgh had the perfect solution. On the first night he took the squad for a meal to an Italian restaurant and the party were split into pre-arranged table plans. Sitting at a table for five were . . . Alex McLeish, Willie Miller, Ally McCoist, Mo Johnston and Roy Aitken. It was the perfect arrangement. Within seconds we were laughing and joking, and it had turned into one of the most enjoyable meals I've ever had. Yes, there were plenty of insults flying, but all good-humoured. Any lingering bad feeling had gone. The Roxburgh touch had done the trick.

The McCoist touch wasn't doing too badly on the inter-national field, either. To be honest, I think my goal-scoring record for Scotland could be better, but, in fairness to me, I've not carried a lot of luck in the dark blue jersey. I've had goals against France and Yugoslavia chalked off for next to nothing, and that is annoying, because goals at that level are prized possessions.

Generally, though, I've been pleased with my overall play as an internationalist and there have been some goals that have delighted me – like the one against Norway that took us to the World Cup finals in Italy and a couple of vital strikes in our successful qualifying campaign for the European championships in Sweden.

I can still remember the thrill of that Hampden goal against Norway that sealed our qualification for Italy. Maurice Malpas powered a header forward, their back four were caught a little square, and I was off and running. Their goalkeeper came out but I lobbed the ball over him, and the Hampden roar had actually started *before* the ball was in the net.

What a moment. People said to me after the game, that I was really brave – that their keeper could have taken my head off. But I have to admit, it never even crossed my mind. All I saw was a gaping goal that had 'Welcome to Italy' stamped across it.

Little did I realise as I danced with delight that Hampden night that Italy would prove anything but a welcoming experience for me.

Chapter Fifteen

ANGRY IN ITALY

THE World Cup finals in 1990 in Italy should have been the pinnacle of my football career – the extra special moment I would always treasure when it came to looking back over my playing days. Instead it left me bitter and disillusioned with an empty feeling of disappointment that I can still recall to this day.

It is ironic, too, that despite all my problems with Graeme Souness, the most heated argument I ever had with a football manager was with the one who had shown me most loyalty in the past, Andy Roxburgh.

But I'm rushing things. Let's get back to the start of what should have been a memorable trip to play against the very best in the world.

As the Scots party began preparing for Italy, I couldn't have been in a better situation. Mo and I had firmly established ourselves as Scotland's strikers and since we had teamed up at Ibrox I felt our partnership had grown in effectiveness. I had scored the goal that had clinched our passage to Italy, and, most important, I felt great. The legs, which had seemed a bit lethargic at the end of some previous seasons, were full of running. Before heading out to Malta, en route for Italy, we had played Egypt at Pittodrie in a friendly. It wasn't a good team performance. We lost 3–1 but I had scored our goal with a good strike.

I felt good. I was mentally and physically at my peak. And I wasn't the only one to think so. We played constant practice games, and the squad defenders that I came up against in these matches, Alex McLeish, Dave McPherson and Craig Levein, were all complimentary. Roll on Italy.

Then the first inkling of a problem. After another practice match, and another couple of goals from me, Alex McLeish, who had been marking me, said: 'That was hard work, Coisty, you were buzzing today.'

But minutes later Andy Roxburgh came up to me: 'What's up with you, Ally?' he asked. 'You were looking a bit jaded out there.'

I assured him I had never felt better, but the first misgivings had started in my mind.

Our opening match was against rank outsiders Costa Rica, and their manager had been quoted as saying that he was really scared of Alan McInally. He said big Alan was 'Scotland's Marco van Basten'. Looking back, the writing was on the wall for me when that was said. I think the Costa Ricans pulled a con trick, and Scotland fell for it.

Maybe that's being unfair to Andy Roxburgh. Maybe he had always intended playing Alan against Costa Rica. I'll never know. All I can say is that I don't think I have ever been so sharp in my life, and here was Andy telling me I was jaded. Believe me, every footballer knows when they are not 100 per cent, and I am no exception.

Perhaps Andy had already decided that Johnston and McInally were to be his opening strikers, and he was looking for reasons to drop me. Whatever the scenario, I began to get very bad vibes about my participation in the opening game.

Then came the big moment – the morning of the Costa Rica match and the team announcement, and even that turned into a bit of a farce. Andy took the five squad strikers aside for a private talk – myself, Mo, McInally, Durie and Fleck, and said he was sorry but he was only playing two of us – Mo and N'ally, an abbreviation on McInally! And I misheard him. I thought he said 'Mo and Ally', so I actually thought I was playing. 'What was all the sweat about, Ally?' I said to myself, suddenly very happy with life.

Andy continued to talk about how we were to play, and I saw that assistant coach Tommy Craig was looking at me very quizzically. Of course, he was thinking, 'My God, Coisty's taking the bad news well.' Then, all of a sudden Coisty wasn't so happy. Instead of saying, 'Mo and N'ally', Andy said, 'Mo and big Alan', and I realised I wasn't playing.

I was absolutely gutted, and very disappointed in Andy Roxburgh, firstly that he didn't pick me, and secondly that there was no word of explanation as to why I was dropped, no hint of a warning.

Now I wasn't asking for special privileges, but Andy is a great squad man. He must have known that I would be totally devastated by his decision. Even if he had pulled me aside before the meeting and given me a ten-second explanation of what was about to happen, it would still have hurt, but maybe not as much. I felt, rightly or wrongly, that I was owed that much.

The plan was that the squad would go for an early lunch, have a couple of hours kip, then head off to the stadium for the game. But I wasn't for eating. I went upstairs to my room and phoned my dad back in East Kilbride with the bad news. He said all the right things – not to worry, that it was only for one game, that I'd be back in the team for the Sweden match. But despite all his kind words, it was a very depressed footballer who sat on his bed, doing a crossword book and thinking the world was a mighty cruel place indeed.

Of course, by one of those bizarre twists which football throws up, my room-mate was Alan McInally. Now you can imagine how our spirits had changed in the past couple of hours. From not thinking he would play, Alan was in the team. For me it was the opposite. As my morale had plunged so his had soared.

From out in the corridor came the unmistakable sound of big Alan – heading for our room, and very, very happy with life. He was giving out this loud, exaggerated hum of delight – the kind of madcap, zany behaviour that makes the big man great fun to be with – normally!

'Hummm humm, hummm, humm, humm, hummmmmmmmm,' came the voice down the corridor and into the room. 'Humm, humm hummmmmmmm,' he continued, then stopped and glared at me sitting on the bed, head disconsolately buried in my crossword book. 'Oi, you,' he snapped at me. 'Get that light out. Some of us have got a game today.'

Well, it was cheeky, outrageous, typical McInally – and just what I needed. For the first time since the team announcement, I was laughing again. It still hurt, and still does for that matter, but the big man had proved the ideal tonic.

To be honest, I don't think I'd have got through Italy if I hadn't been rooming with Alan McInally. He was the perfect antidote for depression, always wanting to laugh, always seeing some light relief, no matter the gloom. And he had his share of disappointment, too. After the 1-0 defeat by Costa Rica, Alan was dropped for the Sweden game, and there he was, mirroring my actions of a few days earlier. He was phoning his dad for some words of encouragement – lying on his bed wondering what had gone wrong with the world.

Having given me no sympathy, he certainly wasn't getting any back. On the day of the Sweden game, as he lay there glaring at the ceiling, I threw him my crossword book and said, 'I guess you can help me with them today.' He loved it, but then anyone who gives out as much as him has to be able to take it.

I mean no disrespect to Alan, but I think if I had played against Costa Rica, Scotland would have beaten them. Alan is a superb player, but the Costa Ricans were ready for our high ball tactics that day, and it suited them down to the ground.

By that stage, I like to think Mo and I had a special understanding. We were playing well together for Rangers, and I think we would have given the Costa Ricans much more to think about. Also, with Mo and I up front Scotland would have played the ball on the deck far more than they did on the day, and that wouldn't have suited Costa Rica.

I know all this sounds like sour grapes, but I can't believe that Mo and I, publicly acknowledged to be Scotland's top strikers a few months earlier, didn't get the chance to face the minnows of the group. There were goals to be had there. But the only goal of the game came from the Costa Ricans and that left us a mountain to climb when we went back to Genoa a few days later to face Sweden.

By which time I was ready to throw myself off a mountain. I had been overlooked again, and this time I was blazing mad.

Once again the bad vibes started before the team was announced. Andy Roxburgh planned to tell us the side after a morning training session. But as we arrived for the work-out, all the press photographers there had one request – they wanted pictures of Mo and Robert Fleck, posing together.

'Surely not?' I thought, fearing the worst. 'But why did they want the picture?' There was something going on, and a sick feeling started growing in the pit of my stomach.

When the team was announced, it was even worse than I feared. Mo and Flecky were playing up front, but Gordon Durie was on from the start, too. I was on the bench.

I was pulverised, totally gutted. From joint first choice striker out of five, I had gone to fifth choice – without kicking a ball.

I asked to speak to Andy Roxburgh privately after training, and the lads had a long wait on the bus as we exchanged some very angry words in the centre of the practice pitch. I was doubly outraged. I hadn't been picked again, and the press had seemed to know about it before me. That was unacceptable. It got heated – very heated indeed.

At one stage, Andy turned on me and stuck his finger in my face. Now I'm not an aggressive man at all, but I told him if he didn't remove his finger, I'd stick it somewhere he wouldn't like!

It is hard to explain my emotions then. I felt let down, badly let down. But in some strange way it seemed as if I had let all my family and friends down by not making the team. It sounds crazy, but that's how it appeared to me.

Andy insisted that he felt I was jaded, not 100 per cent McCoist, and I couldn't, and still can't, agree with that. But he was the manager, he had made the decision, and although it left me with an empty feeling that I'd never had before, I had to accept it. When we left the practice field and headed back to the bus, it certainly wasn't the most amicable of partings, but there was no way either of us could hold any grudges. I think we have too much respect for each other.

Our fall-out was one of those things that happen in football. They are inevitable when 22 players are chasing 11 highly prized places, and once they have blown over, they have to be forgotten.

One thing Andy certainly convinced me of that day was the fact that he hadn't leaked our team plans to the press. He gave me his word on that and I don't doubt it for a second. But when I phoned my dad to give him the latest piece of bad news, he wasn't that astonished. He told me that all the papers back home had been speculating on a Johnston-Fleck striking duo, and, surprise, surprise, it turned out they were right.

That proved to me that someone, not Andy, in the Scottish camp had let the cat out of the bag, and that was wrong and very bad for morale among the players not selected. I can't say what annoyed me more – being left out of the team, or finding out that others knew before me.

So, once again, I found myself sitting on the bench in Genoa, though this time watching a much more enjoyable Scotland performance. The lads did really well against Sweden – 90 minutes of positive football that surprised the Swedes and delighted the huge Scotland contingent in the stadium.

With big McInally encouraging us, the Scotland bench joined in the fans' fun. We leapt up when the 'wave' passed our part of the ground, and laughed uproariously at every opportunity. To the outsider, it must have looked as if we were having great fun, but the smiles were all superficial. Deep down we were hurting and desperately wishing we were part of a committed Scotland performance that was giving us a 2-1 victory and a chance of qualifying for the later stages of the World Cup for the first time ever.

Now all that stood between us and a place in the knock-out stages was a team called Brazil, the same Brazil that had totally played us off the pitch on our own Hampden Park a couple of years earlier. We had lost that game 2-0, but only required a draw against them in Turin to reach the later stages. And strange as it seems, I don't think Brazil were particularly bothered about beating us that night. They had already virtually sealed their own qualification, and I think were quite happy to play the 90 minutes away in Turin and not pick up any injuries. There was never the same intensity about their play that I had noticed in the previous game at Hampden, and that had been only a friendly.

Of course, the starting line-up against the Brazilians that night had featured yours truly. I wasn't arguing about that selection though I did think to myself that if I was too jaded to play against Costa Rica, how the hell was I sharp enough to face Brazil?

I had a real job lifting myself mentally for the game. Scotland punters will be amazed at that. 'How can a Scotland player not be fully motivated to play a vital World Cup game against Brazil?' I can hear them asking. I had just taken a mental pounding. Not being picked for the Costa Rica and Sweden games had given my ego a real battering, and, as you'll have noticed, that's not an easy thing to dent. Don't get me wrong, when the whistle blew, I was off and running, giving it my all, but it wasn't enough. At the very top level in football, the saying is that the first yard is in your mind – i.e. you are moving to a spot before you know it. I have to admit that wasn't happening for me that night.

So my only starting game in the World Cup finals ended in disappointment as I was hooked off and had to watch in horror as a late Brazilian goal, and a miraculous save from their keeper off Mo, saw Scotland lose 1-0 and face almost certain elimination.

But being Scotland there was still a slight mathematical chance that results in other groups the following night would let us scrape through. Also, of course, being Scotland, these results never materialised, and we were out.

I remember sitting with some of the lads in a café-bar watching the games that would decide our fate. We were on edge, hoping for a miracle, but when the games were over and we were definitely out, mega-depression set in immediately. I would have walked straight to the airport from the bar. I wanted to go home, see my family and friends and put the whole experience behind me.

Over two years later, the memory of Italy is still with me. It is like an operation scar, not painful now, but it will never go away – a reminder of an unpleasant experience.

Looking at the situation positively, Italy taught me some important lessons – like never to take anything for granted in football. You never know where the next threat to your position will come from. Italia '90 showed me I had to be tougher. It made me a bit more resolute, and that stood me in good stead when things began to go wrong at Rangers the following season.

But, overall, Italy was a negative experience, and I'm glad to say that I've not had too many of them in my football career. You can only take so many. It dented my Scotland allegiance, but in no way diminished it. You don't play for Scotland for the money. You play for the prestige, and the honour.

Well, I didn't have much of that in Italy, but when the qualifying campaign started for the European Championships, it never crossed my mind to join those of the Italy squad who had decided their Scotland days were over. The dark blue shirt still means too much to me, and I was delighted to play my part in taking Scotland to their first ever European finals.

The World Cup still beckons. If Scotland are to make the 1994 finals in the USA, they have to prove their worth in a tough section that includes the might of Italy and the dangerous Portuguese. I certainly hope to make my contribution in these qualifying games, and if I were to grab a few goals perhaps a place in the squad for the 1994 finals wouldn't be an impossibility. I'll be 32 when they come around, and strikers of that vintage have proved their worth in previous finals.

Italy should have been the highlight of my international career and it wasn't. America shouldn't, but perhaps it may yet prove to be. Whatever happens, I'll be there, either trying my heart out on the field, or singing myself hoarse on the terracings.

Roll on America!

Chapter Sixteen

UNDER NEW MANAGEMENT

WEDNESDAY, 4 September 1991, and there was no scoring so far in the Skol Cup quarter-final against Hearts at Tynecastle. Then it happened. Mark Hateley rose above the Hearts defence and nodded the ball on to me. I had managed to steal a yard from my marker and I was away. A good strike and the ball was in the net. Final score, 1-0 Rangers.

A good goal, by no means the best I've scored in my time, and certainly not the most vital as far as Rangers were concerned. But when I think back now, it was possibly *the* most important goal of my career, the one that sparked off a chain of events that led to me pledging myself to Rangers for my career.

Season 1991-92 was so good for me that it is easy to forget just how badly it had all started. The groin injury which had plagued me for the last three months of the previous season had been finally diagnosed as a hernia problem. A three-second examination by a Harley Street specialist had located the damage. He had stuck his pinkie in the appropriate spot. And what a jolt of pain – they had to scrape me off the ceiling.

But I was a bundle of mixed emotions as I recovered in London from the operation. There was relief that at least the problem had been solved, but worry about how long it would take me to get back to full fitness. The lads were due to start pre-season training shortly, and I knew I wouldn't be able to join them.

After the trials and tribulations of the previous season prior to Graeme Souness's departure to Liverpool, I was well aware of just how important the forthcoming year was. I couldn't afford any more setbacks, and here was one straight away. Pre-season training is a vital part of any footballer's year, and straight away I would be lagging behind my team-mates. How quickly could I catch up?

The Ibrox management and backroom boys were magnificent. I was trying to run before I could walk, and they were careful not to let me overdo things and cause myself even more damage. Physio Bill Collins gave me a lot of gym work, and assistant manager Archie Knox realised how important it was for me, psychologically, to feel part of the team. Archie encouraged me to train beside the rest of the lads as much as possible. Although I couldn't do the same heavy work as them, at least I was there enjoying the patter. I was able to go with the team to the training camp in Italy, and by the end of the spell there I was beginning to catch up with them.

As well as the physical side of things, my mental attitude was being nurtured. Although he had just arrived at the tail end of the previous season, Archie knew all that I had gone through. We had some long chats, and I knew that at some time I would get my chance in the team, and it was up to me to take it.

That opportunity looked like presenting itself immediately. After a couple of warm-up games, Walter and Archie told me that I would be playing in the opening League game of the season – against St Johnstone at Ibrox. I was delighted, but it was short-lived. On the day before the game, I pulled a thigh muscle in training, and was out. Not only that, but Rangers played magnificently to win 6-0 and Mark Hateley and Mo Johnston got five goals between them. Here we go again, I thought.

And, yes, that was me back on the bench again – and nothing I could do about it. But unlike the previous season, I felt that under Walter and Archie I *would* get a chance, and it would be a fair chance. And unlike the previous manager, I *could* talk to Walter about the possibility of me having to leave Rangers.

After a few games on the bench I asked for a meeting with

him, and put my side of the case. I told him that I realised the team was playing well, and that I didn't expect him to change it for me. But I was coming up for 29, and I couldn't afford another season like the previous one. I had to have first team football for the sake of my career, and although I didn't want to leave Rangers, I would have to start thinking about it seriously. I told him, too, that despite all the problems I had never said that to his predecessor.

Walter was just superb – there is no other word for it. He said he understood my frustrations perfectly, but that he didn't want me to leave the club. He appreciated, however, my service to Rangers, and in return he wouldn't stand in my way if I really wanted to go. But he stressed again that I would get my chance, and not to do anything hasty for a couple of weeks. We agreed to sit and think things over for a spell.

Walter was as good as his word, and my opportunity came soon afterwards, that night at Tynecastle. It was my chance, and I took it, literally. That goal got me back in the first team, and I was off and running. I went from substitute to first team regular, the goals started flowing and I had a season I'll never forget.

Far from leaving Rangers, the next chat I had with Walter Smith about my future was to sign a contract that tied me to the club for the rest of my career. What a change in a few months.

But what if that ball hadn't hit the net at Tynecastle. If it had flown over the bar or hit the post and stayed out, would that have been me back on the sidelines with the inevitable question marks about my long-term Ibrox prospects? I've never asked Walter or Archie, so I'll never know, but, looking back, there is no doubting the significance of that goal that night.

Not that it did all that much for Rangers. We were knocked out of the Skol Cup in the next round, losing to Hibs in the semi-final, but that Hampden defeat was the only real blemish on some great performances.

Of course, the team had changed quite a bit in a relatively short space of time as Walter's influence was seen. Andy Goram, Dave Robertson, Stuart McCall, Dale Gordon and Alexei Michailichenko had all arrived. It was Walter's side. And although our style of football hadn't changed that much since the departure of Graeme Souness, there was a different atmosphere about the club.

A bit more relaxed. Less hassle, more laughs. Here was a style of football management I could really relate to.

A perfect example came when we played Hibs in a midweek League game at Ibrox. We struggled in the first half and were 1-0 down at the interval, but we got things going after the break and won 4-2. It was a good night. I got a couple of goals, one a really good strike from a free kick. I ran to the touchline for a typically subdued McCoist celebration. And who was first to hug me? Archie Knox – who had leapt from the dugout to join in the fun.

Can you imagine the lift this kind of spontaneous gesture gave me? From having a manager who couldn't get off his seat to clap when I scored a goal the previous season, to one who wanted to run on the park to congratulate me.

As you'll have gathered by now, I'm no shy introvert. I'm loud and demonstrative and appreciate the same exuberance in others. It's the way to get the best from me – the carrot rather than the stick, if you like.

Not that I didn't get my rollickings that season, too. Walter and Archie weren't slow to let me know if they thought I wasn't doing enough, and I didn't have any problem accepting any of the flak that came my way. In their case I was sure the criticism was to make me a better player, the team a better unit. Criticism from the previous manager was getting personal, with little justi-fication.

Why, Graeme Souness had even lambasted me one day when I *hadn't* been playing. The team had lost 2–0 to Hibs and I poked my head round the door at full-time, just as Souness was conduct-ing an angry post-mortem. He saw me and, ignoring all the players who he thought had just let him down on the park, started on me – I was all the useless so and sos under the sun. What I had done wrong sitting in the stand, I'll never know. But after experiences like that, it wasn't too hard to take the odd knuckle rap from Walter and Archie, and I'm glad to say there weren't too many of them.

Not that we deserved too many of them. I was really pleased with my play that season. I felt that Mark Hateley and I were the best striking team in Scotland and that Rangers were by far the best team in the country. I was pleased with my own game, and had the feeling I was going to score in every match. Having that confidence in yourself is half the battle for a striker.

There were other plus points during the season, too. Once he settled down to the pace of the Premier League, Alexei Michailichenko proved an absolute delight to play with. I know he has his critics, but you'll not find me among them. He has got great vision and is such a gifted passer of the ball that if I make a run, no matter how awkward or unlikely the pass is, he'll find me. That's good to know.

And the biggest bonus of all, for the team in general and me in particular, came towards the end of the season with Ian Durrant back to his brilliant best in the first team.

Deep down, I never doubted that he would make a full comeback, but I must admit there were times I was scared for him. It gave the squad a great lift at an important part of the season rather as if the management had gone out and signed another £3 million player. He had some outstanding performances on the park, and it was good for morale to have him back at his chirpiest in the dressing-room – he has got the second best patter in the team!

So we progressed rather smoothly towards another title. There was one major hiccup late in the season when Celtic defeated us 2-0 at Ibrox. We were dreadful that day, but with hindsight it wasn't such a bad thing to happen to us. We had a few points to spare in the title race, but that defeat was a reminder to everyone that League titles have to be won, not strolled to, and our attitude was a lot better for the remainder of the season.

The game that clinched the title was a good example, a 4-0 victory over St Mirren. We didn't play particularly well in the first half, but I scored one just before the interval and that set us up nicely for the second half. We really turned it on after the break and could have notched more than the three goals we added. I got another one, thanks to my wee mate Durrant. He gave me a through ball and went for the return. That was supremely optimistic of him, as I had no intention of passing, but his run took a defender away, and I turned and fired home. I was pleased with that one.

And so we celebrated another League title, number five, and

a very special one for me. I was pleased with my contribution to the effort – I had scored some important goals along the way.

After the doubts and despair of the previous season, I was delighted too with my overall form, and being named Player of the Year by Scottish Football Writers' AND the Professional Footballers' Association was a remarkable contrast to 12 months earlier.

I was thrilled, too, for Walter Smith and Archie Knox. Basically, players go out to win matches and championships for themselves and their team-mates. This time I genuinely wanted to do it for Walter and Archie, and I took as much pleasure in their delight as I did in my own.

The celebrations went on long into the night, and the next morning. If I were to tell you that at 5.30 a.m. on the Sunday, Andy Goram and I were sharing a bottle of champagne at the bottom of my garden, you'll get a rough idea of the party spirit. Andy and I have booked the garden seats for the same time, same place next year, and, hopefully, for the next few seasons after that.

You can't beat that winning feeling, and there's nothing about the Ibrox set-up which suggests for a moment that it is going to stop. That's why there was little hesitation when, during the middle of last season, I was offered a new deal with Rangers. Although my present contract still had two years, Rangers wanted to sign me up for life, and I didn't take much persuading. I'll now finish my career at Ibrox, and that's fine by me.

I have to admit that deep down there is a twinge of sorrow that I never gave Europe a try – a slight regret that I'll never know how I would have done playing for one of the big continental outfits. But these feelings are more than compensated for by the realisation of what I have achieved at Ibrox and what Rangers are capable of doing in the near future. Rangers have grown enormously in my time there. I can only see them getting better, and I'll be there to play my part.

That will do nicely for me!

Chapter Seventeen

A DAY IN THE LIFE OF A RANGERS PLAYER

I'M wide awake and a glance at the clock in the bedroom in Glasgow's Moathouse Hotel confirms that pre-match nerves are definitely getting to me. It's only seven-thirty a.m. and normally on match days it would take an earthquake to stir me before nine o'clock. But this is no normal match day.

It is Saturday, 9 May 1992, and Cup Final day. The Scottish Cup, the one domestic trophy that has eluded Rangers despite our success of recent years. The Scottish Cup, a story of disappointments and what-might-have-beens in my years at Ibrox. But not today, definitely not today.

Only Airdrie stand between me and the Cup medal I've wanted since I first kicked a football. Only Airdrie? The media make us overwhelming favourites to win, but that means nothing when you cross the white line and start playing. The same press made Hearts certainties to beat Airdrie in the semi-final and look what happened then. This will be no Cup walkover.

Strange things can happen in this competition. Painful memories of shock defeats by Hamilton and Dunfermline are easy to recall if I choose to, but I am trying to keep these thoughts well buried. This is a day for positive thinking, not negative fears.

I glance across at my room-mate, Ian Durrant, still dead to the world – and not a pretty sight. Sleep had not come easily the previous night. We had talked well into the small hours of the morning, unable to get over. The talk hadn't been particularly football, just anything to quell the nerves. Eventually we had both dropped off and I find out later that Ian had wakened up at five in the morning to turn off the telly, which had still been on.

So he sleeps on, and I lie back and resurrect some happy memories of Rangers' path to Hampden that season.

It couldn't have been a harder start – away to Aberdeen at Pittodrie. It was anything but a classic encounter but the most important thing was the result, 1-0 for us. I got the goal, too – not a great goal. What am I saying, they're all great goals? Let's just say it wasn't one of my all-time greatest strikes of a ball, but it was enough to beat Theo Snelders on the night. That, plus a magnificent save by Andy Goram from Brian Irvine late in the game, saw us safely through to the next round and a meeting with Cup holders Motherwell at Ibrox.

That was Alexei Michailichenko's day. He really got us out of jail then. Motherwell were brilliant for the first 20 minutes and Phil O'Donnell had shot them ahead, after I had helped by heading the ball straight to him (stop that, Ally, you're having negative thoughts again!). But two goals by Alexei gave us a 2-1 victory. A lot of the press thought Motherwell had been really unlucky, and, yes, they had played well. But coming back from 1-0 down to win against a team in form takes a good performance. We had done well.

Next round, and another difficult away tie, this time against St Johnstone at McDiarmid Park. We had struggled there in the past and expected a similar tussle this time. But in the end we turned in one of our best performances of the season and ran away 3-0 winners. I had hit the post early on, then put us ahead with a good back-post goal after great work by Peter Huistra. That settled any early nerves and we just blew St Johnstone away that night – a great display.

And that had brought us to the semi-final, and Celtic at Hampden. What a game that had turned into. In terms of passion, commitment, pleasure and importance that must rank among the top six games I've ever played in a Rangers jersey.

Losing Davie Robertson early on – I couldn't believe it when I saw the red card – had really put us up against it. But that's when this Rangers squad had shown exactly what they are made of. We re-organised superbly and played as well and as bravely as I can remember any Rangers team in my spell at Ibrox.

It had been bitterly cold, difficult wet conditions, but I know we gave the Rangers fans plenty to keep them warm. And I had scored a goal that I'll treasure for ever. Just as half-time approached Stuart McCall and I had broken upfield. He had squared the ball to me and I met it on the run. As soon as the ball had left my foot, I knew it had a right good chance of hitting the onion bag. Gordon Marshall got his hand to it but couldn't stop it crossing the line. I can still remember my shriek of delight as I headed for the Rangers end to celebrate.

That lift just before half-time set us up perfectly for the 45 minutes to follow. Celtic had come back at us, as we knew they would, and had hit the post and the bar, but there was real strength of determination in every blue jersey that match and we had held out for a 1-0 victory.

Looking back, Celtic had contributed to Rangers' resolve in that game. They had beaten us 2-0 in the League at Ibrox a couple of weeks previously, and some of their players had been quoted as saying some very uncomplimentary things about our play and tactics.

Now I don't know if the players in question had said all they were reported as saying – journalistic licence can be pretty liberal, as I've found out to my cost in the past. But what we had read certainly annoyed us and, I think, had contributed to our will-to-win that Hampden game.

What we need is a repeat of that determination today. All that effort will mean nothing if we blow it against Airdrie. But we won't do it. Not today.

Still no sign of movement from Durranty so I creep quietly to the door and pick up the morning papers. Sure enough every one of them has us firm favourites, and that, strangely, makes me even more nervous. I'm a punting man. I know how many odds-on favourites lose every week at the races.

At last, my room-mate stirs and joins me in reading the papers. And straight away the patter is flowing.

Dave McPherson, at that time with Hearts but now, happily, back at Ibrox, has done the pre-match assessments for one of the papers. Durranty can't believe that he has only been given a rating of 8, while I have got 9½. I tell him that I was only getting marked out of 9½, while his is obviously a percentage. We're off and running.

It is not nine o'clock yet, and we decide to go down for breakfast, another sure sign of pre-match nerves. Normally, Ian and I never see the breakfast room on match days, but Cup finals are different, as we are finding out. There is no one from our party there – we have beaten the entire squad, with one exception.

John Brown has already been and gone. Bomber's pre-match nerves are legendary. He can't sleep before a big game and is invariably up at first light.

There are constant reminders that this is a special day. Fellow guests in the hotel normally just smile and nod to us, but today they come up to our breakfast table and wish us all the best. One or two hopefuls even ask if there are any tickets going spare, but that really is wishful thinking. As with every big game, finding enough tickets for family and friends has been a real problem. I think I have done well, but if I had doubled my allocation there still wouldn't have been enough. All the lads will tell you the same. In fact ticket queries are so bad that the gaffer asked the hotel to ban ALL incoming calls for the Rangers squad from Friday night to Saturday lunchtime to give us all a break.

The waiter comes to take our breakfast order and I realise I don't want anything to eat, but I order some tea and toast to keep my room-mate company.

There is no point eating now as I will be having a pre-match meal of poached eggs and beans on toast. I never used to take anything before a game, but a couple of months ago I had the exact same order at lunchtime on a Saturday, and scored two goals. Since then I've always eaten the same meal, and the goals have continued to flow. Superstitious? Yes, and no way do I plan to break the spell today of all days.

Before coming to the Moathouse the previous night, we have had two days preparation down the Ayrshire coast at Turnberry. The message from the gaffer and Archie has been consistent right through. Airdrie can't win the Cup. Only we, the Rangers players, can stop ourselves from winning.

Yes, we've been analysing the Airdrie players and their expected formation, but Walter deliberately does not want us thinking too much about them. He wants us to concentrate on our strong points. Man for man we are a better team than them. If we play to our potential, we will win. If they throw us out of our stride, upset our rhythm, suddenly it's a whole new ball game.

Airdrie have had some nasty things said about them in the press, some criticisms they don't deserve. They are a physical team, yes, no doubt about that. But they are not a dirty team, no worse than many others. But they will mark us tightly, try to frustrate us, and hit on the break. That is their only chance. I think everyone, even the Airdrie players, know that if we can get the first goal the Cup is on the way to Ibrox.

We have gone over the Airdrie defence and we expect big Gus Caesar to pick up Mark Hateley, and Walter Kidd will be detailed to look after me.

The gaffer doesn't have to tell me much about Walter Kidd. I've played against him many times, and know what to expect. He is a wily campaigner who knows all the tricks. He will stick to me like glue, and basically make life as difficult as possible. Tackle-wise, Walter has his moments but generally I'm expecting a hard but fair tussle with him.

Mark and I have talked about it and we both know that given the normal run of the ball during the match we will get our chances. It is up to us to stay cool, wait for them to appear and take them.

Breakfast time over, Durranty and I go for a walk round the hotel, and we still can't find any of the other lads. I really hate this time. I'm nervous, but trying to pretend I'm not. I'm just desperate for the action to get under way, but as usually happens in those situations the time is really dragging.

Of course, we still don't know the team, and that in itself has sparked a bit of controversy. Before dinner the previous night, Walter had gathered the entire squad together for a brief meeting. Evidently, BskyB television had announced what they claimed to be the Rangers team and substitutes for the final. Walter was furious, and reminded us that he would never have leaked the team to the media before telling us. He wouldn't even say if BskyB had the 13 right or wrong (as it turned out they were wrong), insisting he was saying nothing until the following morning.

The morning grinds on, and at last it is midday and we meet in the foyer for the bus journey back to Ibrox. It is good to be on the move again, even if only for a short time.

Into the Ibrox dressing-room, and Walter reads out the team. It is impossible not to feel gutted for Peter Huistra, who is not even on the bench. He has played in some of the previous rounds, and must have thought he had a good chance of making the 13. 'Sorry, Peter,' I say to him, but he just forces a smile and shrugs his shoulders. It can be a cruel game, this football.

A few more words from Walter, repeating the theme of the week. 'It's up to you,' he says. 'Only one team is going to stop you lifting the Cup and that's yourself.'

Walter is not meaning to run Airdrie down. He wants us to concentrate on our qualities, our assets, rather than worry about what our opponents might do to us.

Just after one o'clock and time to head for Hampden. There has been a pre-final reception for wives, family and friends at the stadium and Ibrox is mobbed, the foyer chock-a-block. That's the last thing I want. I'm the friendliest person in the world, honestly. I'll talk to anyone, anytime – but not before a match. I'm always the same. I just want my team-mates' company in the hour or two before any kick-off, especially today. I don't want to make small talk, so I sit by myself in the dressing-room till the place has cleared a bit and then scuttle on to the bus as quickly as possible.

The bus is a bit quieter than usual on the run to Hampden, another sure sign of nerves. We pass plenty of fans and their reaction, more exuberant than usual, is a reminder of how much this means to them, never mind us!

A great welcome from a good-sized crowd of Rangers fans when we get off the bus at Hampden, and, straight away, we go out to look at the pitch.

Compared to other stadiums, Hampden leaves a lot to be desired, but not as far as the playing surface is concerned. The park is in its usual good condition and I can't wait for the action to start.

Back into the dressing-room and time to get stripped for action. Once again John Brown is living in a different time zone from the rest of us. He is fully kitted out for the game in seconds, absolutely bursting with nervous energy, but the rest of us take a bit longer.

By habit or superstition – a bit of both I suppose – I always leave it to the very last minute before getting changed. I sit about for as long as possible in my blazer and flannels and try to time it that I'm ready at the exact moment we go out on the park for a warm-up.

As I'm getting changed I ask physio Bill Collins for a rub to get some heat into my hamstrings. I don't have any hamstring problems at the moment, but after a spell of trouble with them a few years ago, I like to look after them.

Richard Gough wants some similar treatment from Bill, and that amazes me. I point out that it is only players with real pace that have hamstring worries, so he must be imagining it. As ever, he takes the stick in good part.

Out on to the park for a warm-up and a real roar from the fans.

The place is filling up quickly. I'm conscious that there are some five-a-side games going on, but I couldn't tell you what was happening in them. It is just good to get a kick at a ball and expend some of the pent-up energy that has been building up for days.

Back into the dressing-room, and the final words from Walter and Archie. Each player is getting an individual pep-talk, but generally speaking the message is the same. 'Go out and do your best. Enjoy the occasion. Stay calm. Keep your composure even if it stays 0-0 for a long time. You'll get your chance.' That's the constant theme.

Time to head out to the park. Mutual wishes of good luck are exchanged, then we file into the tunnel and stand side by side with our opponents. Often in these situations I keep myself to myself, but today a bit of banter seems the ideal way of lifting tension.

As part of their pre-match build-up one of the TV stations had taken some wives of Rangers and Airdrie players to lunch and filmed them chatting. Allison had been there and she had said the wives had all got on famously. I spot Evan Balfour, whose wife had been one of the Airdrie representatives there, and I start giving him a bit of stick about how it was disgraceful that the Airdrie women had let my wife pay for the meal.

It's a good icebreaker. The Airdrie boys seem cheerful and relaxed. They are obviously going to enjoy the whole occasion, and that's a good philosophy for them.

There's a longer delay than normal in the tunnel. Gary Stevens is replacing a stud at the last moment, but eventually we walk out to a real Hampden welcome. It's a spine-tingling moment, a mixture of pleasure and nervous anticipation.

As we line up for the presentation, I try to spot my mum or Allison in the stand, but that's a waste of time. It's only two-fifty-five, there's no chance they'll be here yet. Punctuality is not a great family trait.

Hand-shakes over, and a great roar from the Rangers end as we run down there for the final shoot-in. As ever, I warm up with Andy Goram, chipping shots at him to give both of us a feel of the ball. But, as usual, I always hit the last one past him into the net. The superstitions aren't over yet, either. As I turn to go up to the centre circle, I put my chewing gum out on the penalty spot – don't ask me why, but it has worked all season and I'm not stopping now.

The game gets underway, and now that the action has started all trace of nerves has gone. I glance round at the Airdrie formation, pretty

125

much as we expected, with Gus Caesar picking up Mark and Walter Kidd looking after me.

Walter is quick with some patter. 'It's good to see you sober, Ally,' he quips, a reference to the previous Sunday when I had received my Player of the Year trophy from the Scottish Football Writers' Association. That dinner is always a good night, and winning it had made it an even better occasion this year. It's a huge event, and to be honest, I don't even remember meeting Walter at it. But I say, 'You were in some state yourself', and it was a good guess as he just laughs ruefully.

He has plenty to be happy about on the park. Airdrie have started well, better than we wanted them to. They are hustling and bustling, and we can't get into our normal pattern.

Then, after a few minutes, we break upfield and I get an early ball just outside their area. I get a good touch on it, swivel and lose Walter, and try to chip John Martin. That doesn't work, but overall I'm pleased with the effort. It's an encouraging start.

Airdrie continue to give us problems. They actually get a couple of half-chances, but thankfully don't take them. Our bench is not a happy place. I can see Archie shouting and bawling and pointing, but unless you go across to that actual wing you can't hear what is being said.

No messages of complaint are being passed to me, so I guess I'm not the target of his anger, but someone is getting it.

But just when Archie is approaching apoplexy, we get the opening goal. Dave Kirkwood slips as he tries to cut off a cross ball, and suddenly Davie Robertson is clear on the left. Mark Hateley makes a front-post run, and I go to the back, which is unusual – normally it's the other way about. But I see the ball coming over, and Mark looks a certainty to score.

I try to keep myself steady in case he misses the ball or it is saved and rebounds to me. But it's not necessary – he tucks it away. That Scottish Cup is still not ours, but it is getting nearer.

The Airdrie boys look a bit shattered, and I'm not surprised. The goal is a real body blow to them, but they are shouting encouragement to each other and getting back into their game plan. The Cup is not won yet.

Then, just before half-time, we are attacking and the ball breaks to Stuart McCall about 25 yards out. I'm clear on the left edge of the area, and I'm praying that Stuart sees me and hits me with an early ball. He does, and I let it run by me rather than take a touch. Initially

The Blues Brothers. Derek Ferguson and I play for laughs.

Painful memories. No smiles this time as Graeme Souness and I face the press to 'explain' my Cheltenham trip. (Daily Record)

Flashpoint! George McCluskey goes down after a challenge from Graeme Souness, and soon . . .

. . just about every player on the Easter Road pitch gets involved!
(Daily Record)

Well done, Ally. A pat on the back from Souness as I run off the pitch at Ibrox. He wasn't always so demonstrative. (Daily Record)

Cheers! Walter Smith and I pick up our awards. (Daily Record)

Happy together! Andy Roxburgh and I share a laugh during a Scotland training session. (Daily Record)

Special moment. I'll never forget the roar that greeted us at the Rangers end of Hampden as we paraded the Scottish Cup. (Daily Record)

Walter Kidd and I keep on our toes during the Scottish Cup final.
(Daily Record)

We won the Cup! A quick glance at my medal as the Rangers lads
celebrate on the Hampden pitch. (Daily Record)

Scotland United. Maurice Malpas, Paul McStay, Andy Goram, Alex McLeish, Tom Boyd and I show the togetherness that is such an important aspect of the Scots squad. (Daily Record)

Top that! Paul McStay and I pose before leaving for the European Championships. (Daily Record)

Nice one, Brian. I join the celebrations as Brian McClair enjoys his first goal for Scotland – against the CIS in Sweden, 1992.
(Daily Record)

Sitting it out in Sweden. Gordon Durie and I watch the action after being substituted during the European Championships. (Daily Record)

I plan to cut it across the face of the goal, but it bounces at a perfect height, and I decide to have a blast with my left peg.

Like the Celtic semi-final goal, as soon as I strike the ball I know it won't be far away. And sure enough, it skids on the slippery Hampden surface, and bounces over John Martin and into the net. Yes!

Off I go to celebrate. I run to the corner flag at the main stand side of the Rangers end, and I actually zero in on the face of a Rangers fan jumping with delight. It is big Andy Smillie, a pal of Ian Ferguson, and a big lump of a lad – easy to spot. I give him a wave and enjoy the congratulations of my team-mates.

We're 2-0 up. Barring a disaster that is the Cup well and truly won and we all know it.

The half-time whistle goes, and our dressing-room is a very contented place. Walter and Archie know we haven't played that well, but we are two goals up, and that is all that matters. Walter keeps saying: 'Don't let them back into it. Their only chance is to score and hope we panic. Don't let it happen.'

The message gets home. We go out and play a controlled, composed game, though for the purist the second half is a bit of an anti-climax. There is not a lot of football. I have a half-chance when Mark nods a header down to me, but I hook it over the bar. It would have been a great goal if it had gone in, but I'm not too disappointed at the effort.

All the time I am thinking that it is going to take a real miracle goal to get Airdrie back into the game. Although we are not playing well, we are not letting them threaten us either. Even the Airdrie lads seem to have accepted it. They haven't given in, but I can sense they know the game is slipping further and further away from them every minute.

Then they get the lift they have been wanting, and we have been desperate to stop. Their substitute Andy Smith smacks home a marvellous left-foot shot, and suddenly the door that was slammed in their face has opened slightly.

Straight away they have another half-chance, but thankfully this one goes over the bar, and we get the opportunity to compose ourselves again.

I glance over at the bench and see Walter Smith has come down from the stand to make his feelings known. There is a great amount of arm-waving and shouting, but despite the scare, at no time do I think we are going to give up our lead. We are in control. The Cup is ours.

And so it is! The final whistle sounds, 2-1 to Rangers. At last a Cup-winners' medal.

But strangely there is a bit of a lull among the lads in the first two or three minutes after full-time. I think we all know we haven't played well, and that although we have won the Cup we haven't done it with the style we would have liked.

Walter Smith, however, is having none of it. Reminding us of his Dundee United days, he tells us: 'Look, I've played well in five finals, and lost them all. Get celebrating, you've won the Cup!'

And he's right. I look across at the Rangers end, seated now, but still a hot-bed of passion and emotion. The last time Rangers had won the Cup in 1981, I had stood on that terracing and cheered myself hoarse as Rangers had defeated Dundee United 4–1 in a replay. Now I was going to celebrate a Cup win on the pitch. You bet I was!

Up the stairs to collect my Cup medal, a great moment, then on to the park for a lap of honour. I vowed I would never wear another silly hat during these mad moments, but suddenly I'm wearing more crazy headgear and loving every minute of it.

The team are heading down past the north enclosure. I don't know who is holding the Cup at this moment, but I run, grab it, and head up to the Rangers end. Mark Hateley grabs the other handle of the Cup and the roar as we approach the fans is something quite special. What a reaction. I stand and soak it all in, and actually look towards the spot where I'd been in 1981 and remember the hopes and dreams of the teenager who stood there.

I try not to hog the Cup, but I suppose I do. Anyway, someone eventually prises it away from me and soon we are back in the dressing-room, champagne bottles opening, ready to celebrate.

That down moment just after the final whistle is long gone. The fans' reaction shows just how much the Cup win has meant to them. The relief, the pleasure, is just beginning to sink in for the players, too.

There is a long night of pre-planned celebrations ahead for us, and I aim to enjoy every second of it. Soon we are back in the bus for the trip back to Ibrox where a champagne party has been laid on by the club.

But before we go into the stadium itself, the lads, complete with silverware, pay a visit to the Edmiston Club next door. What a welcome. It is like Beatlemania all over again. There is singing, cheering, roaring.

The place is bedlam. They are obviously going to have a good night, and I like to think we contributed to the party mood.

Back into Ibrox for our own reception. The chairman says a few words, the gaffer says a few words, Goughie says a word, well, one or two I suppose, but then he's not into long speeches.

Next on the Ibrox agenda is a party for players and their families and friends. There is a meal, a disco and a band all laid on, plus what looks like a containerload of champagne waiting to be sunk.

But before starting all this, I make a sensible decision. Well, I guess I'm due one now and then. I've heard too many horror stories of players getting so tired and emotional after big wins that they have actually lost their medal. That is not going to happen to mine. I drive back home and see my Cup medal into a safe place. A quick change, and a taxi back into Ibrox. Now the night can really begin, and what a night.

The McCoist family table is right beside the Durrant family, and any slim chance of it being a quiet, sensible evening has gone forever. Allison and her mother, my mum and my sister Alison, know Ian's mother and his brother Alan, so the tables get on famously.

There is an electric atmosphere about the place. Every table is buzzing. There's shouting, laughter, insults flying thick and fast – my ideal evening.

The lads from Wet Wet Wet are there, and we hope to persuade them to join in when the band, Sneakers, come on later in the evening. But before all that, there is a very special detour to be made. My wee mate Durrant has asked if he can make a quick trip with the Cup to his local bar, The District – not far from Ibrox in Paisley Road West. Ian suggests that someone totally dependable and sensible should accompany him on this trip – me. Archie Knox agrees, but only if he can come, too. Graham Clark of Wet Wet Wet joins in, and next minute the four of us are in a taxi making the short trip to the bar.

Now anyone who doesn't know this particular pub will find it hard to imagine just what it was like that night. It is a great Rangers shop, and it was packed with punters celebrating the Hampden result. It was daft enough before we arrived, afterwards I shudder to think.

Durranty asks if he can carry the Scottish Cup inside and off he goes to a roar that would have done justice to a 100,000 crowd, never mind a bar. Next minute Archie and I are up on shoulders being chaired to the front of the pub. We stand on the bar, conduct a few choruses and the singing gets louder and louder. *Graham Clark has witnessed some scenes at his concerts, but even he can't believe what's going on.*

Into the taxi and back to Ibrox with the Cup safely beside us, and by now I'm going for it.

By this time the band are playing, and we decide they need some professional help. The Wet Wet Wet lads? No way. Durrant and I of course. We are up giving it our best shot, and the Wets are soon joining in too. The band are superb, putting up with us all and joining in the fun.

There are some amazing scenes. I'm up there singing, tambourine in one hand, champagne bottle in the other when I glimpse a great sight on the dance floor. John Brown is dancing with Mark Hateley's dad. Why, I'll never know, but I have to abandon my lyrics, I can't sing for laughing.

And so the night goes on. I don't know of any set of players who could enjoy themselves the way we do that night. Some of the English lads have been around a bit, and they can't remember a night like it.

I don't want the Ibrox party to end, but eventually we have to call it a day. Some of the lads are going to carry on into a club in the city centre, but what has gone on couldn't be bettered for me. I'm for home.

By mutual consent Durranty and I agree that our families have been the most outrageous of the night. We take a special pride in that. Top individual performance goes to his brother Alan, but my sister Alison runs him a close second. They've been brilliant.

Outside we pour my mum and sister safely into a taxi for East Kilbride, then Allison, myself and her mother head back home in another cab.

It is one-thirty on the Sunday morning – only 18 hours since I woke up in the Moathouse Hotel? It is hard to believe, so much has happened in a relatively short space of time. But no, it's true. I've now got a Cup medal, and talking about that, my final check before I hit the sack is to make sure that medal was where I left it.

Yes, it's there. In fact, it's been such a good night I think I see four of them. Still as long as there's one there in the morning, that'll do nicely for me!

And there was!

Chapter Eighteen

TOMMY SVENSSON'S BARMY ARMY

THE scene is the European Championship in Sweden – a group match is heading for a draw but the Scots boys are desperate for the winner.

Eventually, it happens. A great move, a magnificent strike and the ball flashes into the back of the net. The Scottish team rise as a man to celebrate and salute our hero, Thomas Brolin, whose goal had made it Sweden 2 England 1.

I have seldom witnessed such scenes of celebration as there were that night in the Scottish team hotel. The 20 minutes from the time that Brolin, now known as Tam Brolin, hit his winner till the final whistle were as riotous and amusing as anything I can remember in my football career.

It may seem strange starting my account of Scotland's European Championship campaign with a game that we didn't play in, but when I think back to Sweden our biggest asset was squad morale and never was it more united than that night.

Now, I am not normally anti-English. I have too many friends and team-mates in the English camp, lads like Gary Stevens, Chris Woods and Trevor Steven. I can remember watching England play their World Cup semi in Italy in 1990 and wanting them to win for the sake of the Rangers boys in their squad. But any chance of similar feelings happening in Sweden disappeared when a TV reporter described how the England boys had been cheering the German goals as they beat us 2-0. That got right up our noses. Allied to that was the fact that the Swedish people had been so good to the team and our fans, and you can see why we were all firmly behind Sweden boss Tommy Svensson and his lads that night.

It was serious stuff. We had organised the usual sweep on the first goalscorer, worth about £100 to the winner. But when David Platt scored for England to earn Gary McAllister the kitty, Gary didn't even clap. He just sat in stunned silence with the rest of us. You could have heard a pin drop. But when Sweden came back into the game, equalised and Tam Brolin notched that great winner, we went berserk. We were doing congas round the room, singing and cheering.

The Ibrox punters sing a song: 'We're Walter Smith's Blue and White Army'. The Scots boys borrowed it that night. We were Tommy Svensson's Barmy Army. I remember big Alex McLeish conducting the mass hysteria. He would shout in a ludicrous Swedish accent: 'We're Tommy Svensson's . . . ' and the boys would yell back 'Barmy Army'. It went on and on, that plus countless choruses of 'There's only one Tam Brolin'.

So the Scots squad celebrated, and I mean the entire squad. We were very much a unit. I have never been with an international set-up which felt so much like a club team, and Andy Roxburgh and Craig Brown take all the credit for that.

I always think that the ideal club set-up is to have a dressing-room where you could easily go for a pint with each and every one of your team-mates. To achieve that at international level, when the players are only together occasionally, is a remarkable feat. Andy and Craig handled us perfectly. It was always a very relaxed atmosphere. The boys were given a lot of free time, and didn't abuse it.

We trained hard and played hard. We also wanted to play for each other, and for the punters. I can't think of another international team that would have come back from two unlucky defeats and win the third 'meaningless' game 3-0 against a side who were still in the competition. But the CIS hadn't reckoned on Tommy Svensson's Barmy Army.

If the World Cup finals in Italy were a downer for me, Sweden was an enormous plus. No, I didn't score a goal, and that has to be a major disappointment for me, but I wasn't the only striker to come out of the competition with a blank. Are you telling me Marco Van Basten is now a bad player? Of course not. Marking was tight, particularly up front, but I never stopped trying. I felt I played my part in three performances that earned Scotland a lot of praise, and I was delighted with that.

As a nation I felt we put far more into Europe '92 than we have ever done before. And we came out of the competition with our heads held high – players and punters alike. Being part of that was a privilege.

The camaraderie, which was like an extra man to us in Sweden, started with our pre-tournament trip to North America. Andy Roxburgh took a lot of stick about this in the media, but his build-up proved totally correct. We played two games, against the USA and Canada, and kept ourselves ticking over for the big challenges that lay ahead.

We also had some great fun. We had some free time in Chicago, and some of us decided we'd have a drink in the tallest building in the world, Sears Tower. At the last minute we discovered it didn't have a bar, but Chicago also has the John Hopkins Tower, the fourth biggest building in the world, and it had a hostelry on the 96th floor. So up we went, and it got a bit silly. It was cocktail hour, so we ordered a selection of everything, the names went in a hat and you had to drink what you were drawn with. They were all pretty tame, apart from Gary McAllister's. It was a tequila-based drink and was actually giving off smoke when it arrived. I'm sure his brilliant performances in Sweden were down to that drink.

The first game of the tour was pretty tame, too – a 1-0 victory over the USA in Denver. Pat Nevin scored a great goal, and it was only their third defeat in 16 matches. But it wasn't a memorable game. It helped blow some of the cobwebs away, but I think we were all playing with one eye on Sweden. The last thing anyone wanted was an injury then.

On to Toronto and a game against Canada. Before the match action, we had a great night at the city's magnificent Skydome, courtesy of a big mate of mine, Brian Budd. He had organised top box seats for a baseball game at the Skydome between the

Toronto Blue Jays and the Minnesota Twins, and we were treated like royalty. What a place.

We got different treatment when the match against Canada started. There were a couple of ex-pats playing for them and they decided they had a bit to prove against us. They dished out a couple of hefty whacks, and we realised we had a far more physical game on our hands than the USA match. But that was no bad thing. We had to roll up our sleeves and dig a bit harder for victory. We won 3–1 and I was pleased to get a goal, after a shot rebounded off their goalkeeper.

Looking back, that game underlined the spirit within the camp. It was very encouraging the way all the lads responded to the physical challenge which had been laid down.

The final match before Sweden was a 0–0 draw in Norway, memorable to me only for an uncharacteristic moment. Did I really try to square a ball across goal to Brian McClair when I was ten yards out with only the keeper to beat? Where was the selfish Coisty we all know? We got real stick in the press for our display, but that just hardened the resolve in the Scottish camp. We were being written off before we set foot in Sweden – very unfairly, I thought.

I'd been very laid back about the whole Championships until the day before the opening game against Holland. Then the whole atmosphere began to get to me. After the disappointment of Italy, I was taking nothing for granted. I was delighted to learn I was playing and in 24 hours would be facing some of the best players in the world, Gullit, Van Basten, Koeman.

But it would be difficult. Gordon Durie and I were playing up front together, but Andy and Craig spent as much time working on our defensive roles in the team as our attacking duties. Koeman and his partner Van Tiggelen are superb defensive players but they are great coming forward too. We had to make sure they couldn't influence proceedings from the back. I think we succeeded in that. When you think of the way Koeman ran the European Cup final for Barcelona, he wasn't anything like as influential against Scotland in Gothenburg.

But, boy, are they tough to play against. They mark very tightly. They have pace and read a game brilliantly. The once or twice Gordon or I got clear, the ball didn't drop for us. Strangely that was mostly to be the story of the Championships for us.

There was one marvellous moment early in the game, when I nutmegged the great Rudd Gullit. I took a throw in from Maurice Malpas, and as I went to return it, knocked it through Gullit's legs back to Maurice. The Dutchman didn't show a flicker of reaction, but I was delighted. I remember saying to Gordon Durie: 'I never nutmegged him, did I?'

The longer the game went on the better Scotland played. Things were tough up front, but I was battling away waiting for the one chance that nearly always will come a striker's way. Not this time, however, and when I was substituted for Kevin Gallacher I was disappointed but realistic. A fresh pair of legs might just have done the trick. Unfortunately, it didn't happen, and I couldn't believe it when Bergkamp stuck Holland's winner away. A 1-0 defeat – we didn't deserve that.

The atmosphere in the Scottish dressing-room was under-standably gloomy. Andy Goram was furious – he hates losing goals. The rest of the lads were more depressed than angry. We had deserved something for our efforts. But there was pride there too. We had shown the critics we could play a bit, we had earned some respect.

Stuart McKimmie and I had been picked to take the custo-mary drug test, and we went along to the medical room to meet the two Dutchmen chosen, Koeman and Van Tiggelen – was I never going to get away from them? They were good lads. As we waited for nature to take its course we shared a few beers and talked about the game. They said some complimentary things about Scotland and admitted they thought the game was heading for a draw till Bergkamp's late strike.

Unfortunately, Stuart could only pass comment, nothing else, and we had to wait and wait. The Scots squad were due to fly to our new base of Norrkopping straight after the game, but the pair of us had to stay behind and fly to join them in the morning. Stuart and I had a meal in Gothenburg that night with Walter Smith. Like everyone else, Wattie thought the boys had done very well and we had nothing to be ashamed about.

We arrived at the team's Norrkopping hotel the next morn-ing. I couldn't get my room door open and had to ask the porter to help. I can still see the look of disbelief on his face when he opened the door and saw what had been done to my room. I had been turned over, good and proper. In my absence, my team-mates had re-arranged my room and possessions. Every bag was emptied and the contents scattered. The bed was upside down. The TV was in the wardrobe. There was clingfilm over the toilet. Even the batteries in my portable CD had been removed and hidden one by one. It was a really professional job. My one regret is not taking a picture of the room as I found it. The porter left in stunned disbelief, and two hours later I had got it almost back to normal. I've got my suspicions who the cuprits were, but in true Charles Bronson vigilante style I decided I would say nothing and would strike back when I was ready.

By now there was a real buzz in the Scottish camp. Our Dutch performance had boosted confidence. We knew we could give the best a game of it, and with a little luck who knows what we could do?

The next task was the Germany game, and Alex McLeish, unable to play because of injury, had watched their 1-1 draw with the CIS. Before we watched a video of the game, big Alex gave us his thoughts on the German team. He was very impressed with their set-up, particularly their defence. However, he thought their one weak link at the back might be Stefan Reuter, whom he hadn't rated at all.

So we started to watch a video of the Germany-CIS game, and the comments began from the lads: 'What a pass from Reuter.' 'Great tackle by Reuter.' 'Magnificent interception by Reuter.' The Scotland team were united in their admiration for the man. Big Alex just sat there and smiled. He loved it. It became a standard joke among the lads for the rest of the tournament. If anyone did something wrong, whether it was in a practice knock-about or the heat of the action against the CIS, the shout would go up: 'Oi, you! You're having a Reuter!'

Stefan, if you ever read this I hope you realise it was nothing personal!

But Alex McLeish took it to extremes. After the first series of matches we had our team of the tournament – picking the best side out of all the performances seen so far. We also had our 'Nightmare Team' of the competition – the side comprising the

11 worst performances we had seen. Alex's team won it. It read – Reuter, Reuter, Reuter, Reuter, Reuter, Reuter, Reuter, Reuter, Reuter, Reuter, Reuter. You can guess who the subs were.

So on to face Germany and until the day I take my last breath I'll never understand that 90 minutes. I don't know how a side could put so much into a match and lose 2-0.

The Germans were big, strong and immensely well organised. I don't think they were as technically gifted as the Dutch, but they put themselves about a bit more. Buchwald and Kohler were their central markers, and they were good – very good.

But Scotland were magnificent that day. Richard Gough, superb against Holland, was even better here. Our midfield controlled vast chunks of the game, yet we couldn't turn that superiority into goals.

The Germans' first goal was a real body blow. It was very well worked and finished, but I still think Klinsmann should have had a foul against him for the way he backed into Goughie as he set the ball up.

The manner of their second goal, a crazy deflection, and the timing of it, right at the start of the second half, would have devastated most sides. The way the team rallied yet again says wonders for the morale Andy had established in the Scotland squad. Critics will say we still lost 2-0 and were out of the tournament, and that's undeniable, but seldom has a scoreline told such a deceiving story.

Stunned disbelief was the only way to describe the dressing-room after the match. We couldn't believe we had put so much into two games and come out with nothing. It was hard to comprehend that we were effectively out of the competition, and hard not to be emotional when we went back on to the park to thank the punters for their amazing support.

I'm delighted to say that everyone who watched the game, Scots, Germans and neutrals, quite rightly lavished praise on the Scotland display. It was thoroughly deserved.

But I was anything but delighted at some of the stick I took about my own personal performances. As in the Holland game, I'd been substituted, always a disappointment. But like that opening match not one chance had fallen my way. I remember speaking to Gordon Durie about it on the way back to the hotel.

Scotland had created an amazing number of opportunities, but not one had landed in front of either of the two main strikers. We went through how we had reacted to different situations, the various runs we had made. They all made sense. But the times we had escaped our markers, the ball hadn't run for us. A fact of life, albeit a painful one.

The bottom line was that Golden Boot Ally hadn't scored in two games, and I was under pressure. I couldn't believe how quickly some of the media turned against me. One minute I was SuperAlly, the football writers' Player of the Year, Scotland's Swedish goal hope. The next I was finished – a has-been who would be lucky to wear a dark blue jersey again.

I should have known how fickle they can be. I should have been ready for it, but I must admit it got to me a bit. Thankfully, the whole atmosphere in the Scottish camp was so positive that it was impossible to be down for too long. The lads soon had me laughing again, not that I didn't take plenty of stick from them. There was a subtle change in the tournament's 'Nightmare Team'. It now read – Reuter, Reuter, Reuter, Reuter, Reuter, Reuter, Reuter, Reuter, McCoist, Reuter, Reuter. A lovely touch – and there was more to come.

The day before the CIS game I woke up to find that a paper back home was carrying a frightening story about me. Under the banner headline 'PLEASE DON'T AXE ME', it had me making an 'emotional plea' to Andy Roxburgh to play me in the final game of the section.

I nearly fell off my bed when I heard about it. This was journalistic licence taken to the extreme. Far from 'making an emotional plea' to Andy Roxburgh I hadn't even spoken to him on a one-to-one basis since the Germany game. But by an astonishing coincidence, as I was lying back trying to soak in this news from home, there was a knock at my door and in came Andy.

He sat on my bed and was quick and to the point. 'Do you want to play tomorrow?' he asked.

'Of course I do,' I replied.

'That's fine then,' he said. 'I just wanted to make sure you were all right within yourself for the game. I'm not going to

name the team until the last minute, but you are definitely in.'
And out he went.

I was very critical of Andy in Italy, so it is only fair that I
set the balance right here. I thought he treated myself and all the
lads magnificently in Sweden. And I'm not just saying that
because he stuck by me. When he walked into my room that
morning I was half expecting him to tell me I would *not* be
playing against the CIS. And I would have accepted that, and
appreciated the advance warning. As it was I was delighted he
gave me a run in that game, and thrilled we gave him a good
victory to end the tournament.

But we didn't do it just for Andy. We were playing for
ourselves, team morale and those magnificent supporters. Before
the final game we went to see them at their camp-site one day –
unannounced and unexpected. What a sight – sweaty armpits,
breath reeking of stale drink, and that was just the Scotland
players. The fans were worse.

No, they were superb. We signed some autographs, posed
for pictures and they cheered us back on to the bus, one by one.
As we sat down for the drive back to our hotel, they started
singing: 'All we are saying is give us a goal . . . '

It was brilliant. But I said to the lads on the bus: 'What about
that ungrateful lot, then. We come all this way to see them, and
all they do is want a goal . . . '

The boys laughed at that, but there was no denying how
much we felt we owed our punters. We desperately wanted to
give them not only a goal, but a victory too. The trip to see the
fans lifted their morale and did ours no harm either.

The lads were getting more and more psyched up for the
game, and I was still taking my fair share of stick.

I had to pass Andy Roxburgh's room on the way to my
own, and there, pinned on his door that afternoon, was a big
picture of me with a bubble coming out my mouth. It said,
'Please don't axe me. Signed The Golden Slipper.' Superb – and
the phantom notice-pinner was to strike again.

The following day the lads were told the team to face the
CIS that night and as I passed Andy's room to go for a pre-match
nap, there was another picture of me pinned to his room door.
This time the bubble said, 'Thank you. You don't know how

much this means to me. Signed The Golden Slipper.' Did I detect Alex McLeish's writing? Probably, but it didn't matter. I went to sleep still chuckling at it, and dreaming of some revenge.

It was a very strange build-up to that final game. We were due to be out of the tournament and flying back to Scotland the next morning. It had been a long haul since that trip to North America, and I think all the lads were looking forward to going home and then on holiday.

We decided we were all going for a night out after the game. Normally we just rolled up for games with a toilet bag, but this time the lads came complete with denims etc. and a change of gear. Tommy Svensson's Barmy Army were going to celebrate.

But first of all we had a job to do. We had to prove to ourselves, our punters, the world's press, scoffing England players – everyone – that we could win matches, not just praise.

The CIS boys couldn't believe our commitment. We played them off the park for long spells and carried that little bit of luck that was missing in our first two games.

Yes, I felt pressure on me that I was expected to score, but I thought it was my best game of the tournament. Their marking wasn't as tight and I saw more of the ball. When Paul McStay's shot hit the post, it was coming right back to me, and if their goalkeeper hadn't put the rebound into his own net I like to think I would have done likewise. I was also delighted with my lay-off to Brian McClair for his goal and really pleased for him when it went in. Brian had been taking far more than his fair share of stick.

The chance I had been waiting for throughout the Championships eventually came my way in the second half. A good ball over from the left, and I had some space on the right of their box. I took a touch and went to blast it, then took another touch round a defender, saw the keeper off his line and bent it round him. It went a touch high and over the bar. It was annoying, particularly for Messrs. McKimmie, McStay and McAllister who had all been waiting for a lay-off from me. I assured them after the game they would have been more worried for me if I'd passed it to one of them!

And that was the European Championships for McCoist. Soon after that chance whistled over the bar I was substituted, and, although no one ever likes going off, I had to admit there wasn't much left in the legs by then. I was glad of a seat and was able to watch in admiration as a Gary McAllister penalty gave us a 3-0 victory and our punters really had something to sing about.

There was a lovely moment on the bench too, when we were able to pass the bad news out to Andy Goram on the park that he had been selected for the drug test. The look of dismay on his face said it all. These tests take time and he knew he would be late to join the after-match party.

And what a swell party it was. We went for a meal and a seemingly endless round of toasts, all proposed by Derek Whyte. We drank to virtually all our own squad, Tam Brolin – naturally, Graham Taylor – strangely, and, in time, to John Logie Baird and Alexander Graham Bell. Don't ask me why.

Then on to a pub absolutely packed with Swedish and Scots punters all having a great time. There was a group playing and next moment Derek Whyte and I were up on stage. I was handed the mike, gestured to the pub in true Bruce Springsteen tradition, said, 'Good evening, Norrkopping!' I've always wanted to do that – and what a roar went up. That was us for the night. I think they needed surgery to get the mike out of my hand, and I could hardly talk the next morning. But it was all worthwhile.

Archie Knox was there, loving every minute of it. 'You've got them in the palm of your hand,' he said to me at one point during the evening. 'Enjoy it, but don't forget pre-season training starts on 17 July.'

And that was Sweden. I'll always look back on it fondly. It's a great memory, tinged with the disappointment that I didn't score a goal. But only slightly tinged – the good far outweighed the bad.

So it was a tired but happy Ally McCoist who flew back from Sweden. Still with plenty of confidence in his own ability, still able to laugh – even at himself.

The Swedish airline had an in-flight magazine which had an advert for nappies or something similar. The ad featured a huge picture of a baby crying. 'Ah well,' I thought, 'if you can't beat them, join them.'

I drew a big bubble from the baby's mouth and filled in the

words: 'Please don't Axe Me, Signed the Golden Slipper'. I passed it back over my head to the rest of the lads and enjoyed their laughter as the plane headed home for Scotland.

Chapter Nineteen

GREAT MOMENTS IN SPORT – 34 OF THEM

IF League titles and Cup wins are the big prizes we all aim for, then individual awards are the pleasant bonuses along the way that lift the ego and do the confidence no harm whatsoever. I've been fortunate to get my fair share of them down the years, and I've appreciated them all – from player of the year honours from various supporters' associations to man of the match awards from game sponsors.

I can't get enough of them. Yes, football is a team game, and the overall success of the side is all that matters. But, if on top of team success, someone decides to highlight your individual performance, even better. We are all in the entertainment business, there to be shot down or praised, and I know what I prefer.

Of all the awards that have come my way, one stands way out on its own – winning the Golden Boot for season 1991–92 as European football's top League goal scorer. It is the ultimate tribute to a striker. We take the stick for the missed chances, and I suppose there have been a few, so we deserve the credit for the ones that go in. No Scot had ever won this before, and I hope more go on to do so, but I was the first, and that felt good. It took a season of consistent goal-scoring to win it – 34 League goals – and I hope you'll allow me a little self-indulgence as I look back at them.

A few words of warning. You are about to encounter a lot

of superlatives. As I said earlier, I only score great goals, some less great than others admittedly, but some so great they almost defy description. Most of them are finished with a superb strike, or a clever touch, and they are all 100 per cent legitimate goals. Accusations of possible handball or offside in any of them I totally dismiss. If these clever referees and linesmen are happy with them, then who am I to argue? And I have absolutely no guilt in claiming those that took a deflection on the way in. If defenders want to stick their legs in front of my shots that's their worry.

So now that the ground rules are laid, let me introduce you to 34 bootiful memories. I hope you enjoy reading about them as much as I enjoyed scoring them:

No. 1: 24 August 1991, Rangers 4 Dunfermline 0. I was substitute, watching the lads cruise to a comfortable 3–0 lead, when I got on for the last ten minutes. There was not long to go when the ball was played back to Ian Ferguson about 22 yards out. He laid a clever first-time pass in front on me, and I managed to steal a yard off my marker, Norrie McCathie.

I took a touch and, as the keeper came out, curled it with my left foot in at his right-hand corner. I was pleased on three counts – it was a good finish (there's a surprise), it was my first League goal of the season and, more important, I had given Walter Smith and Archie Knox a nice little reminder that I could score goals if I got a chance on the park.

No. 2: 14 September 1991, Rangers 1 Dundee United 1. A long ball from Scot Nisbet, or Emilio Butranisbet as he prefers to be called, put me clear with just Freddy Van Der Hoorn to beat. As I turned by him there was an appeal for handball, but I carried on and hit a left-foot shot past Alan Main's right hand. That put us ahead but Duncan Ferguson equalised in the second half.

I watched the game on TV afterwards, and all it showed was that if there had been handball it was unintentional. A word of praise, too, for big 'Emilio', another great lad with marvellous patter. Until he was injured I reckoned he was Rangers' top player for the first four months of last season.

Nos. 3 and 4: 5 October 1991, Airdrie 0 Rangers 4. Another good team performance and two very different goals from me. The first was a diving header, and there aren't too many of them. Peter Huistra did well on the left, and swung over a good cross. I got in front of Walter Kidd at the near post to head home.

If I'm being honest, and it pains me to be so, I have to admit the second was a little bit lucky. Mo Johnston cleverly lifted the ball over a defender to me and I tried to blast home a volley. But I mishit it and that deceived John Martin who was expecting the real thing. It wrong-footed him and went in at his left-hand corner. That certainly didn't stop me enjoying the goal, however. I've no guilt when it comes to that.

Nos. 5 and 6: 8 October 1991, Rangers 4 Hibs 2. I've touched on this game in an earlier chapter. Hibs were 1-0 up at half-time and playing well, but we came back strongly in the second half.

The ball was played back to me and I let fly. I don't know if it was going in, but it took a deflection off Gordon Hunter and went past John Burridge. That, incidentally, was the first of a run of deflected goals against Hibs last season. They really must have loved me.

A shade lucky, yes, but there was nothing flukey about my second. A short free-kick was stopped by Stuart McCall, and I crashed it home with my right from 25 yards. I was very pleased with that one. It put us 3-2 ahead and Peter Huistra sealed it soon afterwards.

Nos. 7 and 8: 12 October 1991, St Johnstone 2 Rangers 3. Young John Morrow made his debut in this game, and did very well, but it was John Spencer who set up my first goal. He had a good dig at goal, and although Lindsey Hamilton stopped it, I was on hand for the rebound.

St Johnstone weren't happy about my second. John Morrow and I broke away and they were wanting offside, but we were in the clear and I was screaming at young John to square it. Thankfully he did, and I'd a simple tap-in. Saints came back to square the game, but big Emilio popped up with a back post winner for us.

No. 9: 19 October 1991, Rangers 2 Hearts 0. A marvellous piece of tenacious play by Gary Stevens set me up for a goal just before half-time. He chased a long ball, right to the byeline. It looked a lost cause, and, technically, he had no right to make it, but he did and cut the ball back in. It caught the Hearts defence sleeping a bit, and I was able to slam the ball in at the near post from six yards. A pleasing goal, but really Gary deserved all the credit. Well, most of the credit. Well, a bit of the credit! Alexei Michailichenko made the two points safe in the second half.

Nos. 10 and 11: 29 October 1991, Dundee United 3 Rangers 2. This was a memorable match for two reasons. Rangers lost, and there weren't too many of them that season, and I scored with a penalty. I struck it well into the keeper's right-hand corner, but it was the last spot kick I notched in the season (after some subsequent misses I lost the job).

The second goal was a good one. Stuart McCall played a clever pass through the middle. United tried to play the offside trap, but I had timed my run to perfection (that's my story and I'm sticking to it) and I was clear. I rounded the keeper and stroked it home. It is not often a team scores two goals at Tannadice and loses. It was a sore one.

No. 12: 2 November 1991, Rangers 1 Celtic 1. This one deserves a chapter on its own – I was very, very pleased with it. For a start it was a great build-up. Mark Hateley did well on the wing and laid the ball perfectly for Gary Stevens. He took a touch, looked up, saw my near post run and chipped the ball perfectly. I had just managed to get in front of Derek Whyte but I saw Pat Bonner coming too, and I knew there would be boots, fists, everything there. Basically I just shut my eyes, dived at the ball and it went off my head into the net.

It was right at the Copland Road end, too, and I remember hugging Oleg Kuznetsov who was warming up at the time behind the goal. Tony Cascarino spoiled my planned night of celebration with an equaliser for Celtic, however.

No. 13: 9 November 1991, Dunfermline 0 Rangers 5. Another impressive team performance and we were already 4-0 ahead, when Peter Huistra sent me clear through the middle. There were some squeals for offside (when will they ever learn?) but I ignored them, rounded Andy Rhodes on his right side and tapped it home with my left.

No. 14: 16 November 1991, Rangers 4 Airdrie 0. I've Mark Hateley to thank for this one. The big fellow had a great game here and finished with two goals. He did very well for mine, too, with a good run down the left and a clever cut back. It actually came at a difficult height for me, and I could have easily whacked it over the bar, but I kept it down well and beat John Martin.

Nos. 15 and 16: 19 November 1992, Hibs 0 Rangers 3. Another stunning performance from big Mark. He scored the first goal and then had a quite amazing lay-off to tee up a chance for me. I blasted it for goal and it hit off Tommy McIntyre and went in. Another deflection but I think it would have gone in regardless.

The second goal was down to Peter Huistra. He broke away down the left and I just had to time my run to leave myself with a tap-in from his cutback. It was very unselfish of Peter. I hope he knows I would have done the same for him in similar circumstances (well, probably).

No. 17: 4 December 1991, Aberdeen 2 Rangers 3. Another virtuoso Hateley performance with McCoist adding a touch of his own. A great team show as well, far better than the scoreline suggested.

Everyone raved about Mark's second goal, and rightly so, when he ran past the Aberdeen defence and crashed home a great shot, but I thought his first was just as good. The ball came at him at a really awkward angle and he did so well to keep it down.

I was really pleased with my goal, too. Big Mark flicked the ball on and it came at an awkward angle to Alex McLeish. He was so busy watching my run that the ball actually hit off him and dropped for me. I glanced up and saw that Theo Snelders was braced for the shot and decided to lob him. It worked and I was delighted. That made it 3-1 and tied the game up for us despite a late scare.

No. 18: 14 December 1991, Falkirk 1 Rangers 3. I got an early goal to set us on the way. Oleg Kuznetsov did so well for me with a strong run forward. I peeled off right and he spotted me. A good near post shot and we were in the lead. I might have missed a penalty here, but we'll just gloss over that.

Nos. 19 and 20: 21 December 1991, Rangers 2 Dundee United 0. Gary Stevens was the provider again. Unusually for him it was an infield run rather than down the wing, but it had the United defence in disarray. He made as if he was going to shoot, then slipped a good ball to me. I saw the keeper coming off his line and curled a right-foot shot past him. He got a hand to the ball but couldn't stop it going in.

The clincher came two minutes from time after good work by Mark Hateley on the right. He teed one up for me on the six-yard box and I just got there before Van der Hoorn and knocked the ball over the line.

No. 21: 1 January 1992, Celtic 1 Rangers 3. What a nice way to spend New Year. My goal was a funny one, a combination of circumstances that left me with a simple chance. It started when Nigel Spackman won good possession in midfield and fed Dale Gordon. The Celtic defence was at sixes and sevens as they hadn't expected to lose the ball and I made a near post run to take a defender away and hopefully set up big Mark. That's what happened. Dale found Mark perfectly but the big man's shot sliced across the face of the goal to where my run had taken me. An easy slide-in and we were ahead.

Although Tony Mowbray pulled Celtic back level, a Hateley penalty put us into the lead and Bomber Brown sealed our victory with a left-peg drive and then leapt over every advertising hoarding in the ground on his way to the Rangers end to celebrate.

No. 22: 11 January 1992, Rangers 2 Hibs 0. An incredible game. Dale Gordon shot us ahead early on and I then proceeded to miss 846 chances to tie up the match.

I could hardly do a thing right, and if I did it was saved or blocked. Eventually, three minutes from time, Nigel Spackman set me up, and my shot was deflected and spun in. I didn't celebrate, just breathed a huge sigh of relief.

No. 23: 18 January 1992, Rangers 2 Motherwell 0. A Dale Gordon shot was blocked and broke to me 12 yards out. I controlled it well and went to blast it, but at the last moment decided to curl it in at Billy Thomson's left-hand post. It just made it, and I was really chuffed. Alexei Michailichenko sealed the game late on.

No. 24: 1 February 1992, Hearts 0 Rangers 1. This was the game that went a long way to clinching the Championship for us. Hearts were our only real title challengers by this time and this defeat knocked them out of their stride.

To be fair, their central defensive trio of Craig Levein, Dave McPherson and Alan McLaren had played me really well. I hadn't had a sniff of a chance, but on average at least one comes per game and I was ready for it. Midway through the second half Dale Gordon headed the ball down to me and I unleashed one of the best volleys I've ever hit in my life. It screamed past Henry Smith into the roof of the net.

I headed for the crowd and gave it the cheesey grin bit in response to Dave McPherson who had been quoted as saying the Hearts players were fed up seeing my grinning face in the papers and wanted to wipe the smile off my face. Not this time, lads!

No. 25: 8 February 1992, St Mirren 1 Rangers 2. I'm sorry, I have to say it, but this was a great goal. Early in the game I got possession wide on the right and headed in. I played a one-two and suddenly I was in their box. Les Fridge came out at me and I flicked the ball from right foot to left and stroked it home, almost in the one movement. My confidence, my touch, must have been sky high to even think about attempting that. I'll not score many better.

No. 26: 7 March 1992, Hibs 1 Rangers 3. A bizarre goal which set us on the way to victory. As the ball bounced around a crowded Hibs penalty area, it eventually came off Davie Robertson's knee. I got my head to it, and the ball somehow squeezed by the goalkeeper and the defender guarding the post. Don't ask me how, I wasn't complaining.

Some would call the goal flukey, even jammy. I'll admit it was a trifle fortunate. Mark Hateley got the other two that day.

Nos. 27, 28 and 29: 17 March 1992, Rangers 4, Falkirk 1. My only hat-trick of the season and one that sparked a late rush of goals as I started wanting that Golden Boot very badly. The first was a nice chip over Ian Westwater, no deflection, honestly, the second a good finish from a great through ball.

The third was, well, hard to repeat. I was through on the keeper, rounded him, but went too far. Suddenly I was trapped on the byeline, with few options. I looked up in vain for a team-mate to come to my rescue, but no luck. There was nothing to do but try myself. The angle was virtually impossible, but I guess it was just my year because it made the net. I tried to pretend I wasn't totally surprised by the end result and had a modest little celebration dance.

Nos. 30 and 31: 18 April 1992, St Mirren 0, Rangers 2. The game which clinched the title for us. I scored our first one just before half-time, and Andy Goram keeps laying claims to this one saying that I never touched it. Nonsense. Andy sent a huge kick deep into the St Mirren half and I saw their central defenders hesitate fractionally. That let me in and suddenly it was just Campbell Money and I. We were both so conscious of what each other was going to do that we both missed the ball, but my momentum was in the same direction as it was travelling and I was left with an easy tap-in.

I mentioned the second goal in an earlier chapter. A great pass from Ian Durrant to me inside their box. His run, looking for the return, split the defence and I was able to turn and shoot home.

No. 32: 28 April 1992, Rangers 1 Hearts 1. A good striker's goal, but to be honest the build-up was even better. John Brown played a one-two with Ian Durrant then stuck a clever ball inside Craig Levein to put Mark Hateley clear on the left. He squared it to me and I scored at the near post. Simple but very effective. A late John Robertson penalty earned Hearts a point in their bid for a Europe place the next season.

Nos. 33 and 34: 2 May 1992, Aberdeen 0 Rangers 2. At last we've come to them, two of the best goals I could ever score, and both on the same day – ten minutes either side of half-time.

The first came when I got the ball out wide and Stephen Wright came in. I nutmegged him, saw Theo Snelders slightly off his line and tried the chip. It worked and I was off and running to the Rangers' dugout.

Because the League had already been won, Archie Knox had reckoned we had let our pre-match discipline slip at the hotel the previous night. I ran up to remind him it couldn't have been that bad. I remember Archie's gruff voice saying, 'Great goal, great goal', then the linesman arrived to give me stick for being off the park. 'Back on to the pitch, Mr McCoist,' he insisted. 'All right,' I replied. 'But it was some goal, wasn't it?' He had the decency to smile.

The second was a long-range shot, and as I swung my boot at it, I remember thinking that it was an outrageous attempt. But I made a good connection and off it flew. Initially I was sure it was just going to hit the post and stay out but it just swerved ever so slightly at the last possible moment and sneaked in at the junction. This time the Beach End of Rangers fans got my full attention as I celebrated.

I was desperate for a copy of these goals and very disappointed to learn that there were no TV cameras there that day. But Aberdeen were having the game videoed for their own private use, and Dons boss Willie Miller organised a special copy for me – a nice gesture and one that proves there is a real gentleman lurking behind that moaning exterior.

So there they are – 34 good reasons why I'll never forget season 1991–92. And although that Golden Boot will rest proudly in my trophy cabinet, I'm well aware that it wouldn't have come near me without the help of my team-mates. It is more than significant that when detailing the goals just about every one of the Ibrox squad assisted with one or more of them – even Andy Goram.

Towards the end of the season all the lads were desperate for me to lift the award. They wanted to do all they could to help me win it. I remember Gary Stevens urging the team on at Pittodrie with that shout. And although it didn't happen, Mark

Hateley had even agreed that if we got any penalties in the last few League games I could take them instead of him.

Mind you, he did say that he would still take any penalties in the Cup final and there wasn't a word of protest from the dressing-room at that.

Talk about ungrateful!

Chapter Twenty

PUBLIC PROPERTY

THE cameras clicked, reporters crowded around trying to get a quote. I was big news again, but this time they were headlines I could do without. The scene was Hamilton Sheriff Court, 1987, and I had just been found guilty of assault and fined £150 after a night out with Ian Durrant and Ted McMinn ended in trouble.

I could go into the rights and wrongs of all that happened that night. I could try to justify my actions. As I saw it, a friend of mine, Ian Durrant, with his leg in plaster from ankle to knee, looked in some danger and I went to assist. I think a lot of other blokes would have acted in exactly the same way if they had seen a friend in similar circumstances. But despite all these thoughts, at the end of the day I was wrong. I was found guilty. I have no complaint.

It was the only time I have been in trouble. It was a humiliating experience which hurt my family. But, looking back, it was also a learning experience, albeit a painful one. It showed that I was public property. Sure, it was great fun being Ally McCoist of Rangers – most of the time. But there were other occasions when it could be anything but enjoyable.

Being a well-known footballer in the West of Scotland requires tact, a thick skin, the ability to laugh off gentle digs and vicious insults. In short, it brings pressures which call on a special sense of decorum. Even the sheriff at Hamilton court that day made mention of the pressures I was under, but it was still no excuse.

Nowadays I would like to think I would act differently in the same situation. Or, to be more exact, I would act differently to make sure the same situation wouldn't crop up again.

Much to the annoyance of my team-mates, I may say, because they loved every minute of the trial. It lasted three days, and each morning the papers carried long reports of the previous day's evidence. At the height of the mêlée, I was quoted as allegedly having said something along the lines of, 'Come here, and I'll really give your dentist something to work on', and that was the dressing-room's favourite line for months after that. If I so much as gave someone a dirty look, there were suggestions that 'he better get his dentist on standby'. Eventually they forgot about it, but it took some time.

Even the fans got in on the act. The trial had to be halted early on the Wednesday because the team had a Skol Cup semi-final against Hampden at Motherwell. I remember the fans at the Rangers end singing, 'You canny jail SuperAlly', all through the game. They certainly weren't going to disown me.

But for a spell it looked as if they weren't going to be seeing much more of me or Ian Durrant or Ted McMinn. The club, quite rightly, were furious. Graeme Souness went bananas at us. We were all being sold, cut price if necessary – he just wanted us out the door.

Eventually he mellowed and the incident passed into history. Time plays tricks with how you remember scenes, but when I think back to that whole scenario now, it is the farcical element I recall – Ian Durrant trying to hobble and run at the same time with his leg in plaster, Ted McMinn with his big John Cleese legs.

Funny? I suppose so, and as they say in the army, if you can't take a joke you shouldn't have signed up. Don't get me wrong, the perks of the job far outnumber the disadvantages. Football has given me a fantastic lifestyle and a trunkful of happy memories that few men will ever equal. I travel the globe, I meet the rich and the famous from the worlds of politics, music and films. It is all fantastic and I revel in it. But when I was a wee boy, I didn't dream of the perks, I only wanted to score goals in senior football. And that experience has been every bit as good as I thought. It is my job to score goals, but when the ball hits the back of the net it still gives me the same pleasure as when I was 14. I love it.

If the price of enjoying all of that is that sometimes I've to grin and smile at some half-wit's insults, then I'm more than willing to pay it. I think maturity has taught me that lesson. When you are 18, 19, 20 you want to take on the world, give every insult a smart answer back. But really that's just taking yourself down to their level.

In my early years at Ibrox, when both myself and the team were struggling, I didn't want to go out if we lost. But in time you realise life must go on, regardless of the 90 minutes that have gone before.

There are difficult moments. You can't play for one half of the Old Firm and not expect to take stick from supporters of the other half. I'm pretty lucky in that I have a good relationship with Celtic fans, in fact at one time they were better to me than some Rangers supporters. But despite that good relationship, you are still going to meet some that will never be on your side. That's life in the West of Scotland. Nothing you can say or do will change that opinion, so why say anything?

Some people are amazing. They'll butt into your company for an autograph and say something like: 'It's not for me, it's for my brother. He likes you, but I think you're crap.' Or you'll have scored a hat-trick that day, but you meet the guy who wants to dig you up about the one chance you missed. I just laugh – it's the only solution.

Allison used to take it harder than me, but she has mellowed too. I feel sorry for her more than me when it happens now. We very often can't go out for a meal together without some interruption.

That's why we always try to have a summer holiday far off the beaten track, well away from the usual European tourist haunts. But even that isn't guaranteed to work. We were in San Francisco last year, relaxing on Pier 39, when I heard the accent from home and the voice asking, 'Aren't you Ally McCoist?' And Ally McCoist switched on a smile and said, 'Yes.' It wasn't difficult to be friendly then, they were lovely people from Nairn, but at other times when the odd insult is coming my way Allison says I am too nice for my own good, and I know she's got a point.

I try to put on the face the public want to see. I want to keep up a good relationship with the kids and the grannies alike. A wee boy asking for my autograph doesn't want to see my face tripping me. He expects a smile. I see no reason why he shouldn't get one.

But the smile isn't a permanent fixture. I have my moods and throw the odd tantrum, and Allison copes with them well. I've known her since my early Sunderland days and we didn't get married until October 1990. Looking back, I wish we had got married much earlier, but we were both a bit wary of marriage – not of each other, but of the huge step and commitment that it meant.

It was a totally unjustifiable fear. My wedding day was the greatest day of my life – hand on heart, it will never be beaten. With my family, and the friends I wanted around me there, I had a fantastic time.

And Allison has been a major steadying influence in my life for ten years now. Marriage has made me a better person. You definitely need someone there for you in your life, and the right someone. Allison is perfect for me. She is not a 'yes' woman. If I'm out of order, she'll tell me, and I need that now and then.

After games Allison and I go for a meal with other players and their wives, and I love it. But before we go for the meal, Allison knows to allow me some post-game indulgence – an hour with the boys, that's an essential part of a match day for me.

Some players get hyped up before a game. I can be pretty nervous in the run up to a match, but I'm always far, far worse after the action has stopped. Don't ask me why. Before the game you are only concentrating on one thing – the match itself. After it's over there are a million things buzzing around in my brain. I should have played an early ball back to Stuart McCall. If only I'd made that front post run a second earlier. I should have hit the ball first time and not taken another touch. And so on and so on. My mind is a whirlpool, and I'm not always good company.

Allison knows to leave me alone at this time. In the first hour after a match, I just want some male company, my team-mates and friends that I know are on my wavelength. Andy Knox, a friend from primary school days, and Cliff Smith, another East Kilbride mate, are at most games, and I see them straight after the full-time whistle. They know how to handle me if I'm still psyched up. I might want to talk about football, I might not. I might be desperate to know how they thought I played. I might be too scared to ask. Either way, they let me steer the conversation the way I want.

That sounds a bit selfish, and it undoubtedly is, but everyone needs their own way to unwind and that is mine. And I don't get it all my own way – Knoxy is quick to tell me to 'shut it' if I get too nippy. In a city packed with back-slappers all waiting to tell me what a great guy I am, I know I'll get no whitewash from them. If I've had a bad game, and I ask for an opinion, I'll get an honest answer – that's good to know.

And that's the truth. People see the easy-going, fun-loving, laugh-a-minute Ally, but I can be moody and crabbit, too.

So the next time someone asks me for my autograph and they get it along with a smile and a few wisecracks, it's not just me they should thank, but also some special friends, and a very special lady.

I know how much I owe them.

Chapter Twenty-One

PLAYING FOR KICKS

THERE is no way you play striker in any level of football and not take some whacks. I've had my fair share of bumps and bruises and, generally speaking, accepted them fairly well. They are part and parcel of the game and you mustn't let them upset you and throw you off your rhythm.

Gary Lineker is the perfect example. I shudder to think of the number of thumps he must have taken in his travels, and I've never seen or heard of him retaliate. That's the hallmark of a real professional. I would like to think that I have behaved as well as Gary, and most of the time I have. But there have been occasions when I've tried to give back a little of what I was taking.

It sounds strange, but it's not the kicks that get me riled. I don't enjoy them, but I can accept them. What can get to me, however, are the sneaky types of bodily contact – the jersey pulling, being held back by the arm. I don't like that. This type of behaviour is much more common in European football than in our domestic game. Maybe it is just as well I never went to a continental club, as I might have found it hard to cope with that week in week out.

Not that Scottish football is for the faint-hearted. Fortunately, I've escaped serious injury on the park but I've had my share of cuts and stitches, and had my nose broken three times. The last was after a clash of heads with Alex McLeish at Aberdeen, and I'd like to thank him for that. My nose had been knocked out of shape with the two previous fractures, Alex actually straightened it that time.

Generally speaking, Scottish football is hard, but fair. The Premier League has some flashpoint moments, but it is not a dirty league. Teams play each other too often now, and it would be far too easy for vendettas to build up if the tackles got out of control.

Unfortunately, that hasn't stopped my involvement in a couple of incidents that I could have done without. The first came back in Jock Wallace's spell at Ibrox when Hearts were the visitors. Dougie Bell hadn't long joined the club and there was a clash between him and Walter Kidd. Suddenly players from both sides were involved and for some bizarre reason that I'll never explain I ran up to join the mêlée and punched big Sandy Clark.

I mean Sandy Clark, my old team-mate, my old room-mate – a good friend. Talk about a brain-storm. Luckily for me things calmed down before Sandy could get his revenge, but the referee sent off Sandy, Walter Kidd and me.

The team was under pressure for not playing well. I was getting stick for my performances. Perhaps these facts contributed to my behaviour. Whatever the reason it was inexcusable.

I got a fearful bollocking and a hefty fine from big Jock immediately after the game, but as far as Sandy and I were concerned the incident was over. We actually met and had a couple of beers together that night. He came along to the Bellahouston Hotel, and there was a mark near his eye where I had caught him. But he wouldn't even give me the credit for that, insisting he had got it at training on the Thursday night. We ended up laughing about the whole matter, which is how it should be in those situations.

Unfortunately the Scottish Football Association didn't see the funny side of it. As well as our automatic one-game bans, we were all suspended for three more matches and given a stern warning about our behaviour.

Because my disciplinary record had been so good until then, I appealed against this extra ban. But far from helping me, it nearly went against me. The SFA appeal committee actually wanted to increase the ban by another game, to four matches, but luckily for me the constitution wouldn't allow it. I'm sure they had a firing squad in the next room!

That was a warning for me never to get involved in other players' problems, and from then on I kept well away from trouble points – with one big exception.

When Graeme Souness's first League appearance for Rangers ended in mayhem at Easter Road in August 1986, nearly all the players got involved in a centre circle skirmish and I'm ashamed of my part in it. As I mentioned earlier, it was one of the most emotionally charged matches I have ever been involved in. It was a nasty game, played in a bad atmosphere from the first whistle, and as well as Souness being sent off, every player, apart from Alan Rough, was booked for their part in the mêlée.

I'd taken a couple of hefty whacks from Mark Fulton during the game, and when the flare-up started in the centre circle, I decided that was my opportunity to get a bit of revenge with a sly, little dink at him. Of course the TV cameras caught me in the act, and showed it for what it was – cheap and nasty.

I can laugh now at the Sandy Clark flare-up, put that down to a little bit of hot-headedness. But I'm really ashamed of the Mark Fulton incident. It was sneaky and devious. I cringe at the memory.

I doubt if time will ever ease the embarrassment of that one for me, but the years have changed my opinion about another incident that, at the time, had me livid with rage.

We played Cologne in Europe in October 1988, and it was a real battle. I was being marked, literally, by a big lad, Paul Steiner, and he knew every dirty trick in the book. He kicked me, pushed me, held me. He came up close and tried to pull the hairs on my legs. It was hard going, but the good thing was that the team was playing well, still 0-0 well into the second half with the return leg to come.

I actually had a bit of a chance which I didn't take and they ran up the park and scored. Herr Steiner started giving me some verbals to add to the physical abuse, and I decided enough was enough. So the next time the ball came near us, I had a go at him – all in all a pretty brainless thing to do as it was right in front of the referee, and I didn't even connect with him.

Not that it mattered to the big lad. He let out a shriek and went down rolling in agony. The referee bought it and I was sent off. There was real confusion on the park with the Rangers lads complaining to the referee and the Germans equally puzzled. But as I walked off, sick and furious with myself I heard this voice calling: 'McCoist! McCoist!'

Eventually I looked round and it was Paul Steiner trying to get my attention. He was lying on the ground, supposedly getting 'treatment' but grinning at me, waving and saying 'Bye, Bye. Bye, Bye.'

I had been suckered, well and truly. I was raging with anger at the whole injustice of it. I would have fought the world to get my revenge. But that was heat of the moment stuff. Looking back, the joke was on me and the big fellow deserved his chuckles. I bet he still laughs every time he tells the story, and now, to be fair, so do I.

UEFA weren't laughing, however. They decided my crime merited an extended ban, and despite a personal appearance at an appeal in Switzerland, I was out of the next three European ties. That rather sums up my own and Rangers' recent luck in Europe.

The one cloud over recent successful years at Ibrox is the fact that we've never done it in Europe yet. There have been notable successes, like Dynamo Kiev, and some good one-off performances. I think, too, that we have been a better team than our results show. We've been unlucky, and we've been beaten by teams that weren't rated at the time, but went on to show they had real class.

Last season, for example, we were expected to see off Sparta Prague easily. We played well against them, and should have beaten them, but didn't. But Sparta went on to do very well in the later stages of the European Cup, just losing out in their group to eventual winners, Barcelona.

In 1987-88 we got to the quarter-final of the European Cup and lost out to Steaua Bucharest. We conceded bad early goals in both ties, yet just failed to beat them. Also Graeme Souness had sold Robert Fleck at a very bad time, and I was left as virtually the only recognised striker at the club.

That was our chance that year, I'm convinced of it. We were a good all-round team, and there wasn't a great side in the tournament. With a little luck, which every team needs now and then, we would have made it. But there is no use talking about might-have-beens. We have now won four titles in a row, and although domestic honours are always the first priority any season, we all know we must aim for the biggest prizes and that means proving we can meet and match the very best that Europe has to offer. I'm sure we can.

The European nights at Ibrox are always that bit special, too. There is always a different build-up to the games, a real feel of excitement and anticipation as kick-off approaches. The fans love the atmosphere, and so do the players, believe me.

That's why it is so wrong that the present set-up in Scottish football is doing nothing to aid success in Europe. It is not just coincidence that since these mega-League programmes have come in our clubs' performances in Europe have gone back the way. Hopefully something will be done to put us on an equal footing with the other teams we have to face. It is hard enough taking on the very best with fit, fresh legs. Trying to compete with the AC Milans and Barcelonas when you have played three hard domestic games in eight days just doesn't make sense.

Whatever happens, Rangers fans can be sure that every one of the Ibrox squad is as keen for European success as they are. None more so than Ally McCoist.

And thanks to a very painful lesson from Paul Steiner, I'll be taking my punishment and not going out to exact revenge. Well, not in an obvious way. If defenders get a bit wild, they can often cause their own undoing, as a big Brazilian found out against me a couple of seasons ago.

Brazil came to Hampden for an end-of-season friendly in 1987 and won 2-0. It wasn't exactly friendly early on. At the first opportunity my marker, Ricardo, absolutely smashed me with a tackle. Boy, it was sore. I was still checking all my limbs to see if they were intact when the ball was played up to me again. I knew the big lad was going to dart in front of me to head the ball away, so I just left my elbow there (honest) and sure enough his nose smacked off it as he went to head the ball.

He stood up and gingerly felt round his nose, which was certainly a bit wider than it had been. Then he flashed me a beautiful grin, held up a finger in each hand as if to say, 'That's one each', and offered me a handshake. I smiled, shook his hand and we got back to playing football.

Chapter Twenty-Two

STRIKING PARTNERS

I'VE teamed up with some marvellous players in my time, great passers of the ball, fine tacklers, flying wingers, but the ones who are always that bit special to me are the lads I've played up front with.

Generally speaking, strikers hunt in pairs and good team work is essential. You have to work hard for each other, learn to anticipate what your partner is about to do and establish the kind of understanding that gives you the edge against the defenders marking you. I've been fortunate that since my earliest days in senior football I've been teamed up with some superb players. I know I've learned something from them all – a little piece of skill, a different way of turning or shielding the ball. In some way they all helped shape the player I am today, none more so than John Brogan, my first ever striking partner in senior football.

After a season or so in midfield, St Johnstone moved me up beside Brogie as a stop-gap measure, and it developed from there. John is probably the best ever goalscorer in Scottish First and Second Division football. He has over 200 League goals to his credit, a marvellous achievement. He was the ideal partner for a young player like me learning the tricks of the trade. He was very much the father-figure of our relationship and I watched and listened to him.

John had pace. He was absolutely lightning over the first ten yards, and he could belt a ball too. He was more of a blaster than a placer of shots, but a hard, hard worker. He taught me the importance of stealing a yard on your marker and defenders were often so busy watching him that I got a bit more room. Like many of my striking partners, he did more for me than the other way about.

But while he made a lot of chances for me, John also showed me that every finisher had to have a bit of a selfish streak, too. It was all part of the armoury. So, Rangers fans, next time I've five team-mates waiting for a simple cut back, but instead have a go myself and blast a shot high into the Copland Road stand, don't blame me. It's John Brogan's fault.

In complete contrast to Brogie, my partner up front in my early Sunderland days was Gary Rowell. Unlike John, Gary was a much calmer player, he preferred to place his shots rather than hitting everything flat out. Watching him I learned that, even at the top level, you often have a split second more than you think, and taking that time to aim and place usually pays off.

Gary was one of the best penalty-takers I have ever seen. He had a phenomenal record at Sunderland – something like 16 successful spot kicks in a row. A good player with a marvellous right foot.

And after Gary came the amazing Frank Worthington. Never mind a chapter, Frank deserves a book on his own. What a man! Forget your Gazza or Chris Waddle, I think Frank was the most gifted English footballer that I can remember.

He had astonishing skills. His left was his stronger foot, but his right could make the ball sit up and talk too. By the time Frank came to Sunderland, he had been everywhere, done everything. He was getting on in years, about 63 I think, but boy, could he still play. He used to tell me, 'Get to know the ball. Make the ball your best friend.' He always wanted an early touch in a game. He loved running with the ball.

Frank scored some magnificent goals, but he was more than just a finisher. He could beat men, hit superb passes. He was the complete player.

He was also incredible company off the field. As a reward for escaping relegation one season, Sunderland gave the players a week in Magaluf. My room-mate was Frank Worthington. There I was, a naïve 19-year-old spending a week in Magaluf with Frank Worthington. I was lucky to come out the place alive.

He decided to take me under his wing for the trip. Where he went I went, and boy did he know how to enjoy himself. But the next morning, as I tried to recover from the trauma of the night before, my room-mate had my welfare in hand. He brought me my breakfast in bed, ran me a bath and made sure I was ready for the rigours of another day in his company. Honestly, this morning ritual went on for the week we were there.

My one regret is that Frank and I didn't team up together when we were both at the peaks of our careers. It might have killed me. In fact, you would probably have got only one game out of us, but what a game it would have been.

My first striking partner when I came to Rangers couldn't have been more of a contrast. Sandy Clark – one of the old school centre-forwards, rough and ready but a more honest performer you'll never meet. Sandy was brave to the point of foolhardy. He had more scars on his face than Freddie Kruger, and would put his head where most folk would be scared to go with their feet – a real player's player.

Not the quickest, Sandy made up for that with his willingness to work and take the bumps and the bruises. He was so unselfish to work with, and he taught me one great lesson – never hide. Even when the going was tough and the crowd was on his back, Sandy never took the easy option. He kept battling away, making himself available. I admired that quality in him enormously.

One of the unluckiest players in my early years at Ibrox was Bobby Williamson. He looked set for a long, successful Rangers career but broke his leg in a close season tour in Australia and never quite got the same chance in the team after that.

Bobby had pace, a good shot and there was a hard streak in him too. Defenders can dish it out but they were always wary of Bobby, who could look after himself when the going got tough. He could take the stick, however. I remember him getting whacked against Dundee United and as he tried to run back up the park there was a gaping hole in his grin. He'd had a tooth knocked out but carried on as if nothing had happened.

He had good skills too. He scored the only goal of an Old Firm game with a magnificent overhead kick. It is a great shame Rangers fans didn't see more of him. A good lad.

167

I'll have to emigrate when he reads this, but Colin McAdam was far and away the ugliest of my striking partners. He was an absolute gentleman, well-spoken and tee-total, which is just as well as I would have hated to see him with a drink in him. He was a fearsome sight on the park. One of those players who would run through a brick wall for you – in Colin's case it looked as though he had, a few times!

I remember his first words to me when I arrived at Ibrox. 'You'll need to be thick-skinned to do well here,' he told me, and it was good advice. The Rangers fans were desperate for success and were quick to turn on the team when things went wrong. He was a good, unselfish team-mate and a good friend in bad times.

I was only eight years old when Derek Johnstone scored that famous League Cup-winning goal in 1970. By the mid-'80s we were team-mates when Jock Wallace brought him back from Chelsea.

As with Frank Worthington, I would have loved to have played with Derek when he was a few years younger. As a teenager I watched him score great goals and make them for the likes of Gordon Smith and Derek Parlane, and even in our short time together he set up quite a few for me with his flicks and lay-offs. His ability in the air was phenomenal, but for a big man he had a lovely touch on the ball too. He could score goals with either foot (as you will see if you watch him in action in those flickering Pathé News archive shots).

But it was his aerial power that fans remember. It was a gift, a natural talent that he worked on and improved. I have long since resigned myself to the fact that I'll never have that talent. I have worked on my heading, and I think it has improved. But I'll never be a Derek Johnstone in the air, more Amy Johnstone!

I also watched John MacDonald as a fan on the terracings, then found myself playing beside him. He was a striker's striker, not pretty to watch but effective. He was a poacher, getting on the end of crosses and passes and sending a toe-poke past the keeper.

One lesson I learned from John, and tried to copy wherever possible was his ability to hit the target, no matter the pressure he was under. He nearly always managed to get some sort of effort on range, and that is a great knack. Get the ball on target and it has a chance. Anything can happen. I try to do it every time, honest, I do!

Iain Ferguson had one of the most powerful shots I've ever seen in football, and was a good goal-scorer. It has always mystified me as to why he never really made it at Ibrox. When he and Cammy Fraser arrived in a double deal, Rangers were under real pressure. The fans wanted instant success, and unless the players delivered it they were getting stick – new signings in particular, new strikers even more so.

Fergie scored some excellent goals for Rangers and wherever he went subsequently he always grabbed his fair quota. Perhaps if he had played in a more confident Rangers team he would have blossomed more. I felt he was a better player than he ever showed at Ibrox. One thing I learned from him, however, was never to be scared to have a go from long range if you felt the chance was on. I put a few of those away in my time, and every one brings a really satisfying feeling.

Colin West was Graeme Souness's first signing, and like Bobby Williamson was very unlucky with injury. I had played with Colin at Sunderland, albeit very briefly, and knew what a good player he was. He had a great dig in him, and was very good in the air. A big, strong lad, good to play off. That seemed to be the Souness game plan, play two up front with one feeding off the other.

I think it would have worked. Colin was just settling into the style of the team when he took a horrendous knee injury at East Fife. He was out for months, and by the time he came back Robert Fleck and I were established as the striking duo and scoring a lot of goals together. Colin never really got another chance, and that is desperately unfortunate. The Rangers fans would really have taken to him. He was a big, honest competitor who gave 100 per cent for the cause.

But the man who kept him out was a bit of a performer, too. Robert Fleck was the one who nearly got away. Rumour had it that he was nearly transferred to Dundee for a pittance, and that would have been a tragedy for Rangers.

Robert is very quick and strong, with good balance. He was like a little buzz bomb scurrying about the place. I've one recurring memory of that first season under the new regime at Ibrox. I'd make a short run, and Robert would go long. Big Terry Butcher would spot Robert's run and ping a great left-foot ball over the top to him. We worked that so often that season. Sometimes he would make the short run, and I'd go long, but the key element of course was big Butch's ability to spot us and hit us.

We worked hard at the job. We both had some pace, him more than me admittedly, and we always tried to keep on the move, never give defenders any respite. It paid off, as well. We scored over 60 goals between us and Robert had four hat-tricks that season alone. A good, good player and a fine competitor.

Mark Falco was another Graeme Souness signing in his search for a John Toshack-type player up front. Mark wasn't here very long and never really had a chance to make a lasting impression on the fans, but he certainly impressed me. He had a superb goals per game ratio as a Rangers player, something like 14 out of 18 starts, and you can't argue with that. He was big, powerful, good in the air and had a ferocious left-foot shot.

Mark contributed to possibly the best ever European performance in my time at Rangers – when Dynamo Kiev came to Ibrox in the European Cup and we had to win 2-0. That's just what we did, with Mark and I notching a goal apiece, admittedly two pretty weird goals, and Ibrox going crazy on the night. A game to remember.

Up from England came Kevin Drinkell, probably the hardest worker I was ever teamed up with. What a grafter. He really put himself about. A player's player, but the fans took to him as well.

He was one of the old school. He liked his pint and his fag, and he loved his time up here. I don't think he ever wanted to move back south and it was no surprise when he came back to Scotland to play for Falkirk.

Drinks wasn't particularly tall, but he was very good in the air for his height, and he had marvellous awareness. A pleasure to play with.

Well, Mo Johnston *has* had a chapter to himself, but let me just remind Rangers fans with short memories what a good job he did at Ibrox.

When Mo was with Nantes we were paired together for

Scotland, and he struck me as a magnificent player. I remember thinking wistfully that I would enjoy this pairing every week in club football, and lo and behold, it happened. I'm delighted it did.

Like myself, Mark Hateley took time to settle in at Ibrox. And, as with me, he managed to win over the Rangers fans who were initially against him. That is not an easy thing to do.

To be fair to Mark, I think he had injury problems at Monaco and he wasn't as fit as he wanted to be when he first came here. But since he recovered his sharpness, what a signing he has turned out to be. He is quick, strong and hard. No one messes him about. He has earned the respect of defenders. They know if they give him a dunt, they'll get one back.

But he is not just power and aggression. Mark is a better player than a lot of people give him credit for. He has a lovely touch, he makes good, intelligent runs and he always knows what is going on about him.

The strength of the club was reflected in the fact that Walter Smith could go out mid-season and spend £500,000 on Paul Rideout to increase the depth of the squad.

We didn't play together up front too often in season 1991-92, but I was impressed with what I saw – another hard worker with good skills and great confidence. He showed that in a few games in central defence towards the end of the season. Paul was unfortunate that Mark and I were combining so well for most of the time that he had to wait his turn. I'm sure he'll do well at Everton, if he doesn't room with Mo!

Another two strikers in a similar position are John Spencer and Gary McSwegan, two young lads who had been waiting for their big breakthrough for a couple of seasons now. I always thought their turn would come. They both have too much to offer the game.

Young John is a lovely footballer, tricky, elusive and a good finisher. I'm sure he'll be a good buy for Chelsea. Gary has electrifying pace, possibly the fastest in the club, and he uses it to good effect. It must be very frustrating for him but he has to keep battling away.

I try my best to help and I like to think it does them some good. When I talk to them I can roll back the years and hear John

Brogan saying similar things to a young Ally McCoist. He is a good lad, a good listener. He'll get there.

As well as my fellow strikers at Ibrox, international football has seen me paired with some superb front men. Different talents, different skills, all with some special qualities that have taken them to the highest level of the game.

When I made my Scotland debut back in 1986 in Holland, I was paired up front with Paul Sturrock of Dundee United. There were shades of Kenny Dalglish in the way Paul could turn away from defenders. He was superb at shielding a pass, then letting the ball run through him and wrong-footing the defender breathing down his neck. He scored his fair share of goals, but it is the turning and twisting aspect of his ball control that I always reckoned to be extra special. Every opponent had to treat him with the utmost respect or he'd make a fool of them.

Graham Sharp was another class player at taking a ball and laying off a perfectly weighted pass to a colleague. Although he was scoring a lot of goals for Everton at the time, neither the press nor the fans gave him the credit he deserved, and that was wrong. He always seemed to be fighting for some international recognition, always the player the media said was most likely to be dropped, and the whole hassle got to him, which was a shame. He was as brave as they come, and an ideal partner up front. I thoroughly enjoyed our games together.

I was absolutely delighted that I had a hand in the goal Brian McClair scored for Scotland against the CIS in the European Championships in Sweden. The fans and the media were getting more and more worked up about the fact that he had never scored for Scotland until then. That stopped the nonsense for once and for all.

To be fair, the one person who hadn't been bothered about not scoring was Brian himself. I honestly don't think it concerned him one bit, and neither should it.

Brian is an excellent footballer, a thinking player who could turn out in any position in the team and do a job. That probably contributed to the long run he had without scoring. With Scotland he has been up front through the middle, up front wide, central midfield, right midfield. His versatility was counting against him.

You don't score 30 odd goals in top flight English football

in a season unless you are at the top of your profession. Now that he has broken his international duck, plenty more will follow – wait and see.

John Robertson was unlucky to miss out on Sweden because of injury. As he quickly proved at international level the Hearts man is always liable to get you a goal. He is a goal poacher. He does his best work in the 12-yard area in front of goal. Like John MacDonald, some of his strikes aren't that pretty but they are effective. He is good off either foot, and for a small man he is surprisingly good in the air. Strong, hard, difficult to shake off the ball – a Gerd Muller type.

Gordon Durie is my type of striker – he's not frightened to have a go, from long range or a tight angle if he feels there's a chance, and that's great by me.

'Juke Box' has this ability to play wide on the left, and I don't know if he's all that keen on it. I think he'd prefer to be a down-the-middle striker, and certainly I think he is a marvellous goal-getter. His big asset is that he'll score different types of goals – from brave close-in headers to 25-yard rockets. That makes him so difficult for defences to contain.

Kevin Gallacher was paired up front with me against the CIS in Sweden and I thought we worked pretty well together. Dundee United used him more on the flank than Coventry. He is playing a more conventional striking role for them now. He has great pace, good control and is a clever finisher.

The Rangers defenders won't thank me for reminding them of this, but the Scottish player who gave them most trouble last season was Duncan Ferguson and I'm not at all surprised the big Dundee United lad has made it to the international scene so quickly. He has all the attributes needed to go right to the top. I played with him in Scotland's pre-Sweden tour to North America and was impressed with his attitude on and off the park. His is cheeky, confident and assertive. Do I see a bit of the young McCoist in him?

Possibly, but his patter will never be as good as mine!

Chapter Twenty-Three

GAME FOR A LAUGH

THERE was a howl of rage that made me jump with fright and this huge figure came flying at me, put his big fist round my throat and pinned me to the wall.

You don't mess with Jock Wallace.

The scene was Heathrow Airport in the summer of 1984. Rangers were heading out for a round-the-world tour, and I'd got lost in Terminal 3. A bad start, a very bad start. Big Jock, a stickler for time-keeping, had stormed off the bus in a fury to find me, and when he did, he didn't miss me. What he was going to do to me if I was late again didn't bear thinking about. Breaking my neck and sending me home on the next plane was the least terrifying threat.

I'd never known fear like it, but as I gulped and struggled for breath, I looked over his shoulder and there were my team-mates – three-deep at the back window on the bus pulling faces at me behind Jock's back, trying to make me laugh. If I had so much as cracked the hint of a smile then, I wouldn't be here today, I'm sure of it.

But that's footballers' humour for you. Childish? Sometimes. Infantile? Occasionally. Dangerous? Now and then. But funny? Yes. I love it.

When I look back over the years I think of the characters I've met, the practical jokes, the silly wind-ups, the clever one-liners – all great memories. I like nothing better than sitting down

175

over a few beers with a bunch of team-mates and the stories start . . .

. . . like the time on that same Rangers tour in 1984 when Hugh Burns fell victim to a classic trick. Thanks to my early lapse at Heathrow, Jock was really wound up about time-keeping and there were dire threats about what would happen to the next one to fall foul.

We had just arrived in Australia and everyone was jet-lagged but we were booked to go to a function that night. We had to be in the foyer of the hotel at six-fifteen for a six-thirty departure. I was so scared I was early, and so was Hugh, but as he sat down to wait, he fell asleep in one of the chairs in the foyer. The lads began to arrive in ones and twos, but Hugh didn't stir, he was out to the world.

After a few minutes more, all the Rangers lads hid in a room off reception, and we turned the foyer clock forward 15 minutes. I then shook Hugh awake. 'Shuggie, Shuggie, wake up, what are you doing here?' I shouted at him. 'The gaffer's going berserk. He had to stop the bus at the end of the driveway when he found you weren't on it. You'd better move, now.'

Well, Hugh slowly took in what I was saying, glanced round at the empty foyer, and absolutely flew out the door. I think he passed Carl Lewis on his way down that driveway, only to find out there was no bus waiting. You can imagine the welcome he got when he eventually plucked up the courage to walk back to the hotel . . .

. . . or the time Sunderland were whipped 8-0 at Watford. What a drubbing! I've never known a defeat like it, and to make it worse it was the first day of Watford's new electronic scoreboard – every time a goal went in we had to watch these wee neon figures jumping up and down in celebration.

As you can imagine the atmosphere on the bus home was like a funeral. Eventually we stopped for a break and the manager gave us a few quid to have a couple of drinks and sort ourselves out. Well, we ordered the beers, but no one said anything. We just sat gazing at our glasses. Then Jimmy Nicholl broke the spell.

'Tell you what, lads,' he said in that lovely Irish brogue, 'I felt sorry for those wee electronic fans. By the sixth goal, they

were knackered. They were holding on to each other for support.'
That broke the ice brilliantly, we could laugh again . . .

. . . or another great Jimmy Nicholl story from Sunderland
days. He actually arrived at the club the day of the players'
Christmas party, and we weren't going to let the fact that we
were six points adrift at the bottom of the First Division spoil
our day. A good lunch, a good few pub stops later and we ended
up in a club in the town. The DJ was delighted to see us there
and promptly invited the whole team on stage for a bit of Christmas fun.

The game was pass the foam pie. The idea was that the pie
would pass down the line of players and when the music stopped,
whoever was holding the pie smacked it straight into the coupon
of the guy on his left. A good idea, but the DJ made one mistake.
He gave the pie to me, and I didn't wait for the music to start
never mind stop. Wham, Akkers got it between the eyes, and
that was it – mayhem. There were pies flying everywhere, players
rolling about on stage.

Now Jimmy Nicholl was watching all this. As he had just
arrived at the club, he didn't know too many of the lads and was
a bit reserved about joining in. So Jimmy watched and laughed,
but the guy beside him wasn't amused. A real Sunderland fan,
he was looking for more dedication from his team.

'What about this lot you joined, then?' he asked Jimmy.
'What a shower. Look at them – six points off the foot of the
table, and no wonder. They're a joke.'

Jimmy was having none of it. 'There's only one thing will
save Sunderland from the drop,' says Jimmy, 'and that's team
spirit. Everyone pulling together, and fighting 100 per cent for
each other.

'And that's the way to get team spirit up high,' said Jimmy
nodding to the stage which was now a mess of foam and writhing
footballers. 'If these lads can relax together, they can play
together.'

'You know, you're right,' said the fan, suddenly convinced.
'Go on, Coisty,' he shouted, 'hit him with another pie. Don't
stand there, Venison, get stuck back in at him' . . .

. . . or the time Rangers were on a pre-season tour to
Switzerland and I was a bit late back to the hotel – only 15

minutes or so, but too much for Jock Wallace who was prowling around the door waiting for me and other late-comers.

'Get up to your room,' he growled. 'I'll be up to see you when the rest are in.'

Now Jock is not a man to trifle with when it comes to time-keeping. I rushed upstairs and my room-mate Cammy Fraser was lying back on his bed with not a care in the world, smoking a cigar and watching the boxing from the Los Angeles Olympics which were on at the time.

'I'm in bother, Cammy,' I said. 'Big Jock is coming up here, and I know I'm going to get a slap.'

'Forget it,' said Cammy. 'There's nothing to worry about. He says these things, but doesn't mean them.'

'Cammy, he means this one,' I insisted. 'He is not a happy man.'

'Cool it, son,' said Cammy. 'I'll sort it out for you.'

A couple of minutes later, a pounding at the door sounded the arrival of big Jock. Thankfully, Cammy, my hero, slipped off his bed and headed towards the door, obviously to calm the boss down. Well done, Cammy.

But just as Cammy reached the room door, he took a sharp right turn, went into the bathroom, and I heard the click as he locked himself safely out of harm's way. As I tried to come to terms with this blatant act of cowardice, the room door flew open and big Jock stormed in. I tried to babble some form of excuse, but I got whacked on the jaw and told I was fined. Cammy came out of the loo two hours later when he was sure the coast was clear . . .

. . . or the time Cammy and I were in opposition when Raith Rovers came to Ibrox for a Scottish Cup-tie. He was playing sweeper, and I started the verbals early on by saying to one of the Raith Rovers boys, well within Cammy's earshot, that they must be toiling playing such a fat sweeper. Cammy chuckled, and kept up the patter all through the game. If he just beat me to the ball, I would hear, 'And the fat sweeper's too fast for McCoist again.'

Although Rangers went 2-0 up fairly quickly I hadn't scored, and Cammy was loving it. 'Seventy minutes gone in the game, and still McCoist can't get past the fat sweeper.'

'Seventy-five minutes gone, and where's McCoist? He's in the fat sweeper's pocket.' It was good stuff, and thankfully I got the last laugh.

Late in the game one of the Raith lads tried to clear and it whacked off Cammy and rolled into his own net.

'Eight minutes to go, and still McCoist hasn't scored,' I shouted at him. 'But he doesn't have to. The fat sweeper is scoring them for him.' One of the newspapers published a picture of that goal the next morning and there were Cammy and I both grinning like madmen . . .

. . . or an Old Firm game at Parkhead early in my Rangers career. We were losing 1-0 and down to nine men with Ally Dawson and Davie Cooper sent off. Big Roy Aitken, a lovely man that I've always got on well with on and off the park, decided to have a bit of fun. 'There can't be long to go now,' I heard him say to his fellow defenders.

'Hey Ally,' he shouted to me. 'How long was there to go when you came on?' Now I had been on all game, so this was more than a hint that my presence hadn't exactly been troubling them from the kick-off. I could hear Willie McStay and the others laughing but decided to keep a dignified silence.

Of course the unthinkable happened. Nine-man Rangers came back with a last-gasp penalty, scored by me, to make it 1-1.

Big Roy was raging. 'I still don't know how long there is to go, Roy,' I said to him straight after the re-start. 'But I can tell you the score if you like.' . . .

. . . or another Parkhead penalty incident, this time in the 1992 New Year's Day match when Gordon Marshall tripped me up as I tried to chase a ball.

The referee said a penalty and the Celtic boys weren't happy. As I lay on the ground waiting to get up there were a few of them standing over me hurling all sorts of abuse. I just opened my eyes, looked at them and said, 'Happy New Year.' I think some of them eventually had a laugh at that, but not for a while . . .

. . . or big Roy Aitken, then with St Mirren, trying to give me some verbals when the Paisley boys came to Ibrox towards the end of season 1991–92 with relegation a certainty for them.

He dug me up about a missed chance and I said, 'Big man I need a favour.'

'Sure, what's that?' he asked, all serious.

'When you play Cowdenbeath next season,' I replied. 'Can I get your complimentaries?' That shut him up . . .

. . . or the time we played Dundee United at Ibrox, and as we waited to take a corner, there was the rattle of the substitutes' boards as United prepared to make a change. Mo Johnston glanced over to the touchline and said to Freddy Van der Hoorn. 'That's you off, Freddy.'

There was a muffled Dutch curse and Freddy ran towards the touchline, followed by many more Dutch curses as he ran back – it wasn't his number at all. Wee Mo couldn't stop laughing for the rest of the game . . .

. . . or a great one-liner from Ian Durrant on my wedding day. He was one of my ushers that day and as he drove to the church, he suddenly turned to my mum.

'Jessie,' he said, 'I've just had a great thought.'

'What's that, Ian?' asked my mum.

'Well, it's just dawned on me,' he replied. 'In an hour and a half, I'll be Scotland's most eligible bachelor.' . . .

. . . or another marvellous line from Ian Durrant when I had John Jeffrey and some of the Scotland rugby boys at Ibrox to see a game. I get on really well with JJ, Craig Chalmers and Gary Armstrong and they always look after me if I go through to Murrayfield. This time I was returning the compliment and big John was my guest at Ibrox.

It was a few years after the big man's unfortunate incident with the Calcutta Cup, but Durrant hadn't forgotten. He saw us arriving and, nodding towards JJ, said: 'Coisty, don't let him near our trophy room.'

It was a good line. JJ took it well but later on he pretended to be annoyed and had Durranty pinned against a wall. 'What was that you shouted at me?' he asked.

'It wasn't me,' said a pathetic Durrant. 'It was Derek Ferguson.' . . .

. . . or a quite stunning off-the-field performance from the same Ian Durrant when we played Liverpool in a post-season trip to Israel a couple of years back. The two teams got on very well and ended up having a few beers together one day. Durranty and Bruce Grobbelar were at the bar, chatting and downing beers.

What the wee man didn't know was that Bruce had bribed the barman to slip a tequila into every one of Ian's beers. As you can imagine, he was soon well ahead of the field.

At some time during the festivities I found myself talking to Graeme Souness, Kenny Dalglish and Alan Hansen. I remember thinking to myself, 'This is heavy company, be sure and behave yourself', when into my line of sight came Ian Durrant. The tequila/beers had been working.

He promptly spilled some beer over Kenny Dalglish, which delighted the Liverpool players and then had the Rangers players in fits by tweaking Souness's ears and demanding a better contract. He was brilliant. We were all disappointed when the tequila/beers eventually took their toll and he was carried out comatose . . .

. . . or a lovely moment from a Scotland trip to Rumania. As usual there had been a bit of a card school, and Gordon Durie had taken a hammering. Poor 'Juke Box', I've never seen so many losing hands. But next morning we were driving to training and passed one of these huge food queues that seem a daily ritual over there.

'I wonder what they are queueing up for,' asked one of the lads.

'They're all waiting for a game of cards with "Juke Box",' I replied . . .

. . . and a marvellous moment from the last World Cup finals, although Murdo MacLeod might not see it that way. When we played Brazil in Turin, Murdo was blasted full in the face by a Branco free kick which nearly took his head off.

The funny thing was – Murdo swapped positions in the wall with me at the last moment. I don't know why, I'm just delighted he did.

What a belt! I've seldom seen a ball hit harder. Murdo went down and even after treatment he was wandering around in a daze. He eventually had to go off, but as he tried to recover I shouted across at him, 'Murdo, Murdo, listen to me.' He turned and tried to look at me, but one eye was pointing towards Jim Leighton, the other towards our dugout. 'Murdo, look on the bright side, it could have been a lot worse,' I said to him. 'It might have been me.'

I'm told he laughed at that two weeks later when he came out of his coma.

Chapter Twenty-Four

MY WAY

I'M not in my bath-chair yet, but at 30 it's inevitable that I start looking to the future, to what lies ahead for me, and looking back to the rights and wrongs of decisions that I made along the way.

I wouldn't change much, if anything at all. St Johnstone and Sunderland were important stopping points along the road that brought me to Ibrox, and few clubs in the world have matched the growth of Rangers in the last few years. It has been an exciting place to be.

Yes, there are twinges of regret that I never gave Europe a try. And I'll never know if I would have made it in a successful English side, as opposed to Sunderland who were always struggling in my time there. But I don't lie awake at nights wondering about it.

Should a young professional coming into the game model himself on Ally McCoist? Well, he could do worse. (Do I hear someone fainting in Liverpool?) Looking back, I think I have always been a good professional. In my opinion I've been a good trainer, although some of my managers might have something to say about that. I've tried to enjoy all aspects of training, from the six-a-sides which I love, to the pre-season slog which no one in their right mind would look forward to.

And I've enjoyed myself off the park. No, I wouldn't win any temperance awards, but I've not exactly been Oliver Reed either. Yes, I've celebrated to excess after a good result, but I've never abused drink before a game. If you are doing the business on the park, you deserve to enjoy yourself off the park, too.

To be honest, if it's not happening for you on the park, you'll find it difficult to enjoy yourself off it.

Mo Johnston had a reputation for being a bit of a lad, but to my mind he just enjoyed himself at the right time. And he put the effort in before and after. Never in my time with him did he miss training or even turn up late for it. And few worked harder at training than Mo.

Everyone is different. Some players like to be asleep at nine p.m. the night before a game. Just because I prefer to sit up and talk or watch a film till after midnight doesn't make me unprofessional. What works for some doesn't work for others. It's a question of what's best for you, on and off the park.

The game is changing all the time, even in my relatively short time as a professional, and players must be able to adapt quickly to new ideas and tactics.

The way the game is reported has also altered dramatically in recent years. Young players coming into the game will have to watch how they behave at all times. Certain sections of the media are waiting to pounce on the slightest mistake. That just did not happen a few years ago. I've spoken to Rangers players of earlier eras, the Willie Hendersons etc, and they didn't have the press following them in the same way. Nowadays, you are always under the microscope and I see it getting worse rather than better.

On the field, my advice to any young player would simply be to work hard and enjoy it. I think you can fill kids up with too much technical jargon, when, more often than not, good players know what to do instinctively. And to any young, up-and-coming striker I would say, never be afraid to miss. There's nothing wrong with that selfish streak – shoot all the time even if you've missed your last three. Believe in yourself. It will come good eventually.

But rather than simply give that advice I like to think I'll be around to demonstrate that philosophy for some time yet. Compared with other positions, strikers have an early sell-by date, but others defy the average and keep on playing. I hope to be one of them.

I've thought about getting out at the top, but virtually every ex-player I've spoken to tells me they think they retired too soon, so I'll probably milk every last ounce of energy out my legs.

That's why I've not given the future too much thought. Obviously, Allison and I have talked about how things might shape up, but just vague hopes and ideas, nothing definite. We both love America, and with the game sure to gain momentum over there after the 1994 World Cup, there is always the chance that an opportunity would come up to tempt me over.

Television attracts me. I enjoy being interviewed and I've often thought that I might end up asking the questions rather than giving the answers one day.

At this moment in time, I don't see myself in football management. I suppose that could change, but deep down I doubt it. I would enjoy coaching youngsters – the same mentality, you might say – but I can't see myself as your official team boss giving my side a real Souness-type rollicking. I couldn't get myself as emotionally angry as that.

But the bottom line is that I don't know what to do, because I refuse to think about it.

To tell you the truth, I'm terrified of the end, scared of the day when a manager will put his arm round my shoulder and say, 'Sorry, Ally, we don't want you.' It will break my heart.

I love football, every aspect of it – the excitement, the glamour, the team-spirit, the dressing-room patter, the bumps and bruises – in short the whole ball game. It has been my life for 14 years, and I don't want to imagine myself without it. The day I walk out of a dressing-room for the last time will be the worst day of my life.

So I'll carry on enjoying the best days while I'm lucky enough to be living them. I aim to keep on doing those silly celebratory dances and flashing those big cheesey grins for as long as I can.

I hope you'll all humour me on that one!

. . . AND FINALLY

I GOT to know the McCoist answer-phone message well. His bright, lively voice apologised for being out and, dripping with sincerity, pledged that he would 'get *right* back' to me.

And to be fair he did – usually in a week's time, seldom more than a fortnight.

Mutual friends warned me that helping Alistair Murdoch McCoist tell *His Story* would cost me my sanity, and at times I thought they'd be proved correct. But I survived – just.

Ally and deadlines are a frightening mixture. He lives in his own timewarp, where minutes are elastic, and hours never ending. He speaks his own time language, which I learned to translate only through painful experience. 'You're there, I'll be two minutes,' he would say and disappear into the bowels of Ibrox. Even a slow reader could make a fair indentation into *War and Peace* before he re-appeared.

And if he ever phoned ahead to an appointed meeting place with the immortal words, 'I'm running a bit late . . . ,' I knew there was time to take the family away for the weekend.

There were some bad moments. In the middle of May and well behind schedule, we arranged to do a day's work. It never happened. The author had 'forgotten' the small matter of Scotland's trip to North America. The chuckling voice down the line from Chicago held not a hint of remorse: 'I bet you've lost the last few strands of hair on that dome,' he laughed. 'Don't panic, Crawf. We'll get there.'

And get there we did – just.

To be fair to Ally, when I did get him nailed to a chair with a tape recorder welded into his hand, the professional in him took over. He had amazing recall of games and incidents long gone. He was keen that humorous anecdotes and painful memories were discussed in similar depth. He wanted to tell the full story – warts and all.

If getting him to talk was a pain, listening to him was a pleasure, and I hope we have done his frankness justice in this book.

But what's this I hear? It's a message from Ally on my answer phone, asking me if I want to help him with *Ally McCoist – My Story, The Sequel*.

'Sorry you've missed me, I'll get *right* back to you,' says my message.

That will be right. Where's that Air New Zealand timetable?

CRAWFORD BRANKIN